Acknowledgements

On behalf of the Women's Research Centre I want to thank the many women who contributed to this project. We are especially grateful to our consultants, the women who so willingly and honestly shared with us their knowledge, their analysis, and their passionate commitment concerning issues of violence against women. Thanks, too, to the women who suggested themes to pursue and told us their vision of the "perfect" reading guide. The women who read and so thoughtfully commented on the draft helped us to make it, not perfect, but much better, and we thank them.

As the principal writer I have my own list of thanks owing. Jan Barnsley and Debra Lewis brought a depth of experience and analysis to the developmental work of the project. In the initial review of the literature Andrée Buchanan cheerfully, and to my mind courageously, took on half the books, including the ones I was afraid of. Several other women searched their own libraries for books they thought I should have. Jennifer Ellis and Martha Royea helped with the tedious work of copy editing. My thanks to all these women. Finally, my thanks to the committee, not just for their insights but for their encouragement and support and flowers and pecan squares.

Funding for this project was provided by the Family Violence Prevention Division of Health and Welfare Canada. The Women's Research Centre is solely responsible for the views expressed in this Guide.

Patterns of Violence in the Lives of Girls and Women:
A Reading Guide

Lisa S. Price

Research Committee
Jan Barnsley
Andrée Buchanan
Ruth Chitty
Diana Ellis
Jennifer Ellis
Lisa Price

Women's Research Centre
Vancouver 1989

Patterns of Violence in the Lives of Girls and Women: A Reading Guide

Production Assistance: Jackie Brown
Printed by: Press Gang Printers ® ⟨UNION LABEL⟩ ·41
Type produced by: Eastside DataGraphics
Printed and bound in Canada

Canadian Cataloguing in Publication Data:

> Price, Lisa S. (Lisa Sydney), 1955
> Patterns of violence in the lives of girls and women
> ISBN 0-9692145-6-1
> 1. Abused women - Bibliography. 2. Feminism - Bibliography. 3. Violence - Bibliography. I. Women's Research Centre (Vancouver, B.C.). II. Title.

Z5703.4.W53P75 1989   016.3628'3   C89-091443-5

Women's Research Centre
#101-2245 West Broadway
Vancouver, B.C.
V6K 2E4

Table of Contents

Introduction

Introduction

For twenty years now, feminists of the contemporary women's movement have worked to identify issues of violence against women, to provide services to the women and children victimized by men's violence, and to fight to change the social, legal, economic and ideological conditions which allow such violence to occur. These three aspects of feminists' work are related and have a common grounding: feminists start by listening to women. Feminists believe what women say about their lives-- about their experiences in the past, their needs in the present, their hopes for the future.

Listening to women, feminists named rape as a crime of sexual violence against women, founded rape crisis centres, lobbied endlessly for changes in laws and legal procedures. So too have feminists listened to and spoken out on women's experiences of wife assault, sexual harassment in the workplace, child abuse, especially child sexual abuse, and dating violence. Feminists have also exposed pornography and prostitution as issues of violence against women and are investigating the prevalence and meaning of elder abuse.

Through all this work, feminists have learned a lot about men's violence. Sometimes it seems we know too much--the horror is so much, so various, so unrelenting, so unthinkable. But, of course, it is thinkable and we have an obligation to think it and speak it and continue to struggle to end it.

We have also learned a lot about women's courage and deter- mination and creativeness in overcoming the effects of male violence. We've learned that individual women do survive, that they do emerge from experiences of violence and degradation strong and knowledgable and whole. We've learned that women can and do make the transition from victim to survivor. Women do it every day.

We've learned that by listening to women and speaking and acting on what women say, feminists can create change. We've learned that the work of establishing and running transition houses and rape crisis centres and other support services makes a difference in individual women's lives and in the lives of our communities.

Of necessity, much of our work is quite specialized. Obviously, the needs of a woman sexually assaulted by an acquaintance differ significantly from those of a woman battered by the man she lives with. Feminists have developed specialized services to reflect women's needs. At the same time, though, feminists have been aware of links among the issues. Workers in transition houses for battered women, for example, were among the first to recognize the proportions of child sexual abuse in the families of women who came to the houses. Acting on that recognition, feminists adapted the knowledge and expertise of workers in rape crisis centres, among others, and developed services for victims and survivors of child sexual abuse. Similarly, front line workers are becoming increasingly aware of the common history of childhood sexual abuse among women and children in prostitution and of the prevalence of pornography in the abuse of women and children.

Reviewing our own work in violence against women, particularly wife assault and child sexual abuse, we at the Women's Research Centre began to talk about not just the direct links among issues but overall patterns: commonalities in women's descriptions of their experiences of different forms of male violence as well as commonalities in feminists' analyses of the issues. We wanted to look at those commonalities while still paying attention to the differences among the issues. We believe a sufficient body of knowledge and practical expertise exists among feminists in the late 1980s to make such investigation and reflection possible. And we believe it is essential work to undertake.

By investigating links among issues of violence against women we can better understand how women live, what women experience and what systems of support most effectively meet women's needs. In addition, if we categorize women as battered wives or rape victims or child sexual abuse survivors without recognizing the commonalities of experience among all women, we make it harder for women to speak about the range of their experience and to know they are not alone in being targets of men's violence. By investigating links among issues of violence against women we can better support women's survival. Ultimately, by learning and telling the truth about patterns of male violence we are in a better position to act against that violence.

The work of exploring commonalities and differences among women's experiences of male violence is vitally important. We have prepared this Guide in order to contribute to and encourage the process of theory building, using existing analysis to help us make the connections. Our purpose in this work is to recommend feminist texts which seem to us to give the clearest and most accurate description and analysis of specific issues of violence against women and which add to our understanding of overall patterns of violence in the lives of girls and women. What we present in this Guide is very much a selected bibliography. We have not attempted to survey the field but only to review what we believe are some of the best and truest feminist texts on violence against women.

The audience we have in mind for this Guide is women who want a no-nonsense feminist analysis of specific issues of violence against women and of the commonalities of women's experience. This may include, but is not limited to: students, particularly those in Women's Studies; community women's centres; and front line workers such as rape crisis and transition house workers. For all these groups we hope the Guide will be useful both in providing a perspective on the issues and the connections among them and in providing information to use in their educational work.

To prepare this Guide we began where all feminist analysis begins: with women. We immersed ourselves in women's descriptions of their experiences of male violence. We reviewed and analysed interview material from earlier Women's Research Centre projects on wife assault, child sexual abuse and workplace sexual harassment and from a project on dating violence conducted by Battered Women's Support Services in Vancouver.

This interview analysis gave us three things. First, it gave us what we call a "picture" of women's experience of each of these four issues. The pictures summarize what women commonly describe: what is done to them and by whom, what they think and feel as a result, and what women do to endure, to halt and to survive the violence that is done to them. Second, it helped us to identify similarities and differences among the issues, how raped women and battered women, for example, describe similar experiences and how their experiences are distinct. Third, it told us that many women experience or witness a number of kinds or forms of male violence in their lifetimes. For example, a woman interviewed about her experience of being battered by her husband mentions childhood experiences of watching her father beat her mother and says that her own daughter was sexually abused either by the woman's abuser or by another man. We began to talk about this thread in women's accounts as "constellations" of violence, using the term to describe the various configurations of women's multiple encounters with male violence.

Reviewing what we learned from the interviews, some themes emerged which we formulated as nine statements. These became, in effect, our grounding assumptions or guides to use in developing analysis:

1. It is men who do violence to women: women are the victims, men the abusers.

2. The violence done to women by men is real, is serious, is damaging to the point of life-threatening.

3. Women don't like, desire, need or deserve the violence done to them.

4. Women try to avoid or halt the violence done to them but are hampered in doing so by what women are taught is "femininity."

5. Women learn about men's violence in a variety of ways, starting at an early age:
   i) they learn about violence directly at the hands of abusers, often in a number of forms and a number of circumstances;
   ii) they learn about violence by witnessing men abuse other women--their mothers, sisters, daughters, female co-workers;
   iii) they learn about violence by listening to cultural messages, by hearing the violence done to women dismissed, tolerated, condoned, supported, and even celebrated by the abusers themselves, by friends and relations, by the authorities women turn to for help, and by our society and culture in general.

6. In learning about male violence in these various ways women learn a key lesson in femininity. Femininity describes what women are supposed to be. It includes being weak, passive, vulnerable, and sexually available to men. The femininity lesson women learn through male violence is that women are abusable, that it is normal and acceptable for men to abuse women, and that to be a woman is to be both a target of and responsible for male violence.

7. Women experience different forms of male violence in very similar ways. There are, however, important differences among the issues, just as there are variations in individual experience.

8. Women's experience of male violence may be influenced

by factors such as race, class, culture, age, geographic setting, and mental or physical condition. In particular, the experiences of Native, immigrant and disabled women may be distinct in some respects from the experience of white, Canadian-born or able-bodied women.

9. Men sometimes give reasons or justifications for the violence they do to women, for example that it is a man's right or that the woman is to blame for it. Their reasons are inadequate. The violence done to women by men is inexcusable.

We present these assumptions here so that readers will know the basis for our thinking in developing this Guide, will know what thinking informed our work.

In deciding which issues of male violence to include in this project we were guided by what the women in the interviews said. We also considered the availability of written material and our own need to keep the project manageable. We settled on seven issues which seemed to us the clearest and most closely related issues of men's violence against women and for which we believed there was a sufficient body of literature. (As it turned out, we overestimated the amount of literature on dating violence.) The seven issues are: wife assault, dating violence, rape, child sexual abuse, sexual harassment, pornography and prostitution.

Obviously, this list is not exhaustive. Lesbians, in the face of double oppression, are beginning to speak out about violence in their relationships and to develop community supports for those hurt by their partners. Similarly, feminists continue to describe and analyse child abuse and institutional violence against women (articles on both these subjects are described in this Guide). Elder abuse is an emerging issue--not enough is yet known about the experience of the victims (mostly female) and the behaviour of the perpetrators (mostly male). As important as we know these issues are, we found it was not possible to include them in this project.

Of the seven issues included, we had interview material on all but three--rape, pornography and prostitution. The interviews provided us with a standard against which to evaluate the texts, the standard of women's actual experience of the issues. In the absence of interview material on the other issues, we called on consultants: feminists with a depth and breadth of experience working in the areas, who know many women's stories and were willing to tell us what they know. From their descriptions we developed the pictures of rape, pornography and prostitution.

In deciding which books to include in this Guide we consid-

6

ered a number of factors related to our purpose and our intended audience. Because we speak primarily to a Canadian audience, wherever possible we preferred Canadian books. Similarly, we looked for books which are readable, accessible to a general, non-academic audience. We also wanted books that give a feminist perspective grounded in women's own descriptions of their experiences of male violence.

From our research over the years it is clear that this violence is not gender neutral, that there is a clear gender division between those who do violence and those who suffer it. We looked for texts which recognize this specificity. Throughout this Guide we, along with many of the writers, speak of the violence women and children suffer as men's violence or male violence. In so doing we name the actors--the ones who have the power to choose to use violence, the ones who act on that choice, the ones who rape and batter and in so many other ways sexually abuse and humiliate women and children. To those who say that this naming is blaming we quote American feminist Sonia Johnson: "Telling the truth is not blaming. It is telling the truth."*

Boys and sometimes men are also victims of male violence. Boys are sexually abused at home and in prostitution. Men are raped by other men. In choosing our texts, though, and in reviewing them, we took our lead from the interviews and focussed on girls' and women's experience of male violence.

Finally, because of our interest in patterns of male violence, we looked for texts which discuss direct links among the issues and/or which locate specific issues within the context of anti-woman violence.

We considered all these factors in choosing texts. Of course, we were more flexible about some than others: we have included a number of texts which are not Canadian but only one which is not explicitly feminist.

In focussing on analytical texts we've had to leave out many other useful books. Individual women's accounts, for example, add a great deal to our understanding of women's experience. Similarly, what are sometimes called "recovery" books can be enormously helpful both to survivors of male violence and to their supporters. We have cited a few of these books at the end of each section together with other books we think are worth-while but which don't fully address our subject.

* Sonia Johnson, *Telling the Truth* (Freedom, California: Crossing Press, 1987), p.22.

In calling this a Reading Guide we have two meanings in mind. Obviously, it is a guide to the texts we have listed. But we also want to emphasize that our reading must be guided by women's experience. The pictures which begin each section are descriptions of the issues based on women's accounts. We present them as a framework or reference point for reading. In this work, as in all feminist work, women's experience is the base for questioning, for thinking critically, for uncovering the patterns and hence, for informing our actions against male violence.

Feminism's foundation and greatest strength is its commitment to listening to, speaking with and learning from women. There's something wonderfully exciting about women sitting around a table, describing experience, sparking ideas off each other, discovering threads of meaning and collectively developing analysis. We couldn't invite all the writers in this Guide to our table so we read their books instead. Among ourselves we examined and discussed what they said. Added to the words of the women in the pictures, the writers' words help us begin to trace the patterns of violence in the lives of girls and women. We hope those who use this Guide will continue that process.

conclusion

Picture: Wife Assault

Wife assault, battering, woman abuse--the terms vary but what they are all meant to encompass are violent, often life-threatening attacks by men upon their legal or common-law wives.

Women describe men throwing things at them--a plate of food, a case of beer, a coffee cup, whatever is closest to hand. Women speak of beatings that last hours or days--their husbands kicking them, punching them in the face, slapping them, strangling them to unconsciousness, throwing them down stairs or out of a car, pulling out their hair. The injuries these women list range from black eyes to broken bones, miscarriages, head injuries, knife wounds and on and on. Some women speak of repeated sexual assault as a fact of their married lives. Some women describe being tortured by their husbands.

Many women say their husbands threatened to kill them and/ or their children and often backed up those threats with guns, knives and other weapons. Some say their husbands threatened their security, threatening, for example, to throw the woman out of the family home or send her back to the "old country" penniless. Some women say that while they were beating them their husbands called them names like "bitch." Others describe a constant barrage of verbal abuse: their husbands questioned their intelligence and sanity, criticized their competence in caring for the home and children, and accused them of sexual infidelity.   The women say that it didn't matter that the accusations were groundless, they were still called "slut" and "whore."

Many battered women describe how their husbands kept them isolated, both to increase their control and to keep the abuse hidden.   The means by which the men enforced the isolation varied. Some women say their husbands refused them money and time for social activities. Others remark that their husbands behaved so obnoxiously that friends and relatives stopped visiting. Some were forbidden to keep a job, to go to church or visit neighbours, or even to use the telephone. If they did any of these things their husbands beat them.

For many women living with an abusive husband meant living in a state of constant fear. They say because anything could set the men off, they were unable to predict when the next beating would occur and that unpredictability added to their fear. Some women feared not just the next beating but death. They had good reason to fear, for the abuse to which they were subjected was life-threatening, and their husbands sometimes said they would kill them.

Women don't like being beaten. They describe doing all in their power to make the abuse stop. Some, seeing their husbands' abusive behaviour as a sign of illness--particularly related to alcoholism--tried to get help for the men. They phoned Alcoholics Anonymous, for example. Others, seeing the abuse as a marital problem, tried to get their husbands to agree to go with them for counselling, but most often their husbands refused. Some women say they changed their own behaviour, either to match their husbands' apparent expectations or simply to avoid provoking the men. Since, however, their husbands' standards changed without notice and provocation was never more than an excuse, this strategy too was largely unsuccessful in halting their husbands' abuse.

Finally, many women tried to leave, often repeatedly. Some went to the homes of relatives or friends, or even moved to another city but their husbands tracked them down and forced them to return to the family home. Some say fear for their children caused them to return. Some, still committed to the marriage, returned in the hope "he will change." Many of these women were encouraged to return by police officers, psychiatrists and social workers, who said the woman should "give it another chance." Others were told the violence was their fault and were discouraged from laying assault charges against their husbands. Some women did receive help from professionals, such as a social worker who believed a woman and called a transition house for her. Unfortunately, too many women were turned away when they tried to go to a transition house due to lack of space.

When physical and sexual assault becomes an everyday fact of life women seek ways to endure it. Some tried to just carry on and not think about it. Others actively tried to forget what was done to them. And some women say that deliberately or not, they used alcohol and prescription drugs to dull both the fear and the physical and emotional pain.

Women constantly berated and undermined by their husbands reached a point of believing what was said to them. Some came to think of themselves as stupid, as bad wives and mothers. Some blamed themselves for their husbands' attacks, telling themselves that they didn't try hard enough in the marriage or simply that there was "something wrong" with them. Even after escaping from their batterers some women continued to criticize themselves for getting into the situation in the first place. Others feared becoming victims again, either because of what they saw as some personal failing or because their experience has taught them that all men are violent and use violence to control their wives and lovers.

Women felt great fear of the batterers. For some that fear turned to anger, rarely, a wish to kill. Most women, though, say that even though they were afraid, they felt sorry for their husbands. This is especially true for the women who thought their husbands had "problems" and who tried to help them.

Women's descriptions suggest that the men don't see the violence as their problem. Some women say that their husbands blamed them for the abuse, saying it was the woman's fault or that she provoked or deserved it. In other cases husbands attributed their violence to external causes such as financial worries or claimed to have no control over their behaviour--another way of avoiding responsibility. Finally, many women say that their husbands gave no explanation for their assaults - apparently seeing it as natural and normal for a man to beat his wife.

Based on women's descriptions, what these men seem to expect and require of women is, in a word, everything. They expect women to do and be everything the men want and nothing else. Often this means absolute, unquestioning obedience. Additionally, many women say that their husbands wanted them to be submissive, especially to be quiet in their submissiveness. And some describe how their husbands expected them to fulfill all their needs--from finding their socks to dealing with creditors to sex on demand.

Commonly, women's "failure" to meet these expectations was the "reason" for specific assaults. Women say their husbands beat them when they argued or in any way opposed their husbands' wishes. Sometimes even gentle teasing constituted sufficient "disrespect" to prompt a man to beat his wife. Often women were beaten because they didn't meet their husbands' standards of behaviour or household maintenance even though those standards were undeclared and often changeable: he wants supper on the table then calls the food "slop" and hurls it. Finally and perhaps most tellingly, some women say that anything and nothing was reason enough for their husbands to beat them.

The Texts

Dobash, R. Emerson & Russell Dobash. *Violence Against Wives: A Case Against Patriarchy.* **New York: The Free Press, 1979. 339 pages, indexed.**

In their Acknowledgements, R. Emerson and Russell Dobash thank their editor for urging them to "write about people rather than statistics." We can all be thankful they paid heed, for the text is alive with the voices of 137 women telling their stories in their own words and idiom.

Dobash and Dobash deal with the factual elements of wife assault--the nature of the violence and the injuries women suffer as a result--but they also pay attention to what often isn't measurable--women's responses and feelings about being beaten by their husbands and women's efforts to avoid or divert their husbands' violence. In short, their approach is wholistic and very respectful of the real people they write about. This is not to say that this is a particularly accessible text, for it is very dense and the writing tends toward "scholarism." Still, it gets full marks for a grounded analysis and for making that grounding explicit.

Because they pay attention to what women say, and because they do more than count bruises as it were, Dobash and Dobash can speak with authority on the role (or non-role) of women in wife assault. They are particularly eloquent on the subject of provocation, or "victim-precipitation" as it is known in academic circles. They argue that the notion is both naive and insidious and that it serves to justify men's dominance and control over their wives and to excuse their use of violence. More than simply arguing the point, though, the authors demonstrate how and why it is so. They expose the assumptions that underlie a concept such as provocation and compare those to what is actually happening when a man beats his wife. Though those assumptions are false, they are nonetheless "socialized into everyone," including battered women. Dobash and Dobash record the resulting ambivalence women feel and describe: on the one hand believing they brought the violence on themselves by displeasing their husbands and on the other seeing the injustices done to them and believing they did not deserve to be punished.

At various points in the text the authors take up the subject of how women learn about male violence. They pay particular attention to cultural messages, devoting two chapters to an historical analysis of wife battering and another chapter to the training of girls to be wives. They also discuss at some length theoretical approaches and research on what children learn from observing or experiencing violence in the home. Their argument, in brief, is that while children may learn that violence is acceptable and women appropriate targets by witnessing their mothers being beaten, it is simplistic to assume those children necessarily will grow up to use or suffer violence. They point out that in witnessing or experiencing violence children see not only that violence is an effective means to achieve various ends; they also see the pain and the suffering involved. Dobash and Dobash end this discussion by saying that more and better research is required before any conclusions can be drawn about family cycles of violence. We agree more research is needed, especially regarding the differences in what children learn: boys learn to beat, girls learn to be beaten.

Most of the women Dobash and Dobash interviewed for this study were from Scottish working-class families. Perhaps for this reason the authors do not comment on the influence of race, class, ethnicity, etc. on women's experience of wife assault. Notwithstanding this omission, *Violence Against Wives* is a first-rate description and analysis of women's experience of battering and of the social context within which battering occurs.

MacLeod, Linda. *Wife Battering in Canada: The Vicious Circle*. Ottawa: Canadian Advisory Council on the Status of Women, 1980. 72 pages, not indexed.

In this book Linda MacLeod presents what she calls a "snapshot" of wife battering in Canada. This means it is a brief, but very readable description of the issue based on statistical analysis as opposed to women's own accounts. Particularly because the book was published by an agency of the federal government, it has some public authority and credibility which community-based groups such as transition houses don't have. The very fact that the analysis is largely statistical adds to its credibility. In short, the book is a basic primer, particularly useful for public education.

In sketching out a description of wife assault, MacLeod points out, among other things, that battering is rarely a one-time occurrence, that the beatings women suffer are frequently severe and can lead to death, and that many women are beaten when they are pregnant. MacLeod also devotes some attention to the particular experience of middle and upper class women. She does not, however, mention the experiences of Native, immigrant or disabled women.

Macleod's strongest suit is her social analysis. She succinctly examines the history of the family as an institution and points out those ideological elements which serve to promote wife battering. Among these MacLeod notes in particular women's economic dependence on men, the social acceptance of men's authority over their wives and the resulting acceptance of men's violence against women as normal and legitimate, and the immunity of the family from the laws and rules of society. She also discusses socialization--the training of women in the "womanly" role of supporting men--and how it functions to encourage women to take responsibility for their husbands' violence. She says that the battered woman is supported in feeling guilty by her batterer and the professionals she turns to, and that "she may have learned, particularly if she came from a family in which violence was an accepted form of expression, that battering is part of the lot of women's lives."

We do have some reservations regarding the definition of wife battering MacLeod uses. She says:

> Wife battering is violence, physical and/or psycho-logical, expressed by a husband or a male or lesbian live-in lover toward his wife or his/her live-in lover, to which the "wife" does not consent, and which is directly or indirectly condoned by the traditions, laws and attitudes prevalent in the society in which it occurs.

We find this definition problematic on two counts. The first is its inclusion of gay males and lesbians. While undeniably violence occurs in gay and lesbian relationships, the dynamics involved appear to be somewhat different from those present in heterosexual relationships. Thus, the effect of lumping gays and lesbians in with heterosexuals without differentiation in a definition of wife battering is to create another kind of invisibility.

14

The second difficulty with this definition comes in the phrase
"to which the 'wife' does not consent." This implies that
sometimes women do consent to physical or psychological violence. We consider this an untenable position, even in the case
MacLeod cites of sado-masochism. Indeed, the phrase is at odds
with MacLeod's earlier comment that wife battering "is not
playful, fun or sexually stimulating for the woman."

In spite of these definitional problems, and in spite of the fact
the analysis is not explicitly grounded in women's descriptions,
this is a very usable text, both in its approach and in its format.
In simple, uncluttered fashion it covers the ground, at least in
broad outline. It addresses the basic questions about wife
assault, including myths, and discusses transition houses, police, legal and governmental initiatives from a Canadian perspective.

**MacLeod, Linda. *Battered But Not Beaten
. . . Preventing Wife Battering in Canada.*
Ottawa: Canadian Advisory Council on
the Status of Women, 1987. 181 pages,
indexed.**

This is an updated, and somewhat better review of some of the
issues addressed in MacLeod's earlier book (see above entry).
Perhaps its best to say that while the previous text was a single
snapshot of wife assault, this is more a collage. Most importantly, in this text MacLeod pays attention to groups of women
omitted from her earlier work. Rural women, aboriginal women,
immigrant women, teenaged women, disabled women and women
on military bases battered by their husbands or boyfriends are
all discussed as women suffering "double isolation."

Another change is in MacLeod's definition of wife battering.
The inclusion of lesbians and gay men remains, though it is less
directly stated. The implication that women can and sometimes
do consent to violence has been dropped without comment.
MacLeod gives psychological abuse greater emphasis in her
new definition and in both the definition and the text itself she
stresses that "it is the **persistence** of the violence that estab-
lishes violence as battering."

The statistical analysis presented in the earlier study is
largely replicated here. This analysis likely will prove similarly
useful in supporting and giving credence to the case presented
by battered women's advocates in public education work, fund-

ing applications, lobbying efforts, etc. Statistical analysis, though, is given somewhat less prominence than in the earlier work. In this text MacLeod places greater emphasis on public policy issues surrounding wife assault. Of these the most important is MacLeod's discussion of the changes in the shelter movement over the past ten years and the challenges that movement faces in the future. Though in general her tone in this discussion is that of "objective reporting," MacLeod does argue the need for more, better and stabler funding for both shelter and non-residential programmes for battered women.

Other policy issues MacLeod addresses include services for children of battered women, criminal justice initiatives, and programmes for batterers. Inasmuch as these discussions constitute more than half the text, it is particularly useful to activists engaged in institutional change.

Schecter, Susan. *Women and Male Violence: The Visions and Struggles of the Battered Women's Movement.* Boston: South End Press, 1982. 367 pages, indexed.

Prior to writing this book Susan Schecter spent six years as an activist and worker in the battered women's shelter movement in the United States. That background gives her writing a grounding that a more distanced researcher cannot hope to achieve. Schecter knows the questions to ask and, more importantly, knows who to ask them of--her analysis is based on interviews with former battered women and with movement activists. Schecter's purpose in this book is twofold: to record the radical feminist, grassroots history of the early shelter movement, and to tell the truth about battered women's experience. She succeeds in both precisely because she sees the two as interconnected. She argues that the shelter movement "caused us all to see abused women in a new light," to learn of their strength and ability and capacity for transformation, and hence to discover the inadequacy, if not utter falseness, of psychotherapeutic models of battered women.

Given her background, it is not surprising that Schecter provides a very clear description of the abuse inflicted on women by their male partners--not just the beatings, but the rapes and verbal assaults as well. She also discusses what battered women do to try to end the violence and the obstacles they encounter, particularly, of course, the violent man and his unwillingness to change his behaviour.

In analysing why men batter Schecter looks at domination,

control and power within the family and, just as importantly, looks at the social imperatives which support and perpetuate men's violence. She argues that these imperatives--the legacy of patriarchy and the requirements of a capitalist economy--result in sexist socialization which trains men to abuse and women to accept responsibility for men's abuse. Throughout this "theory-building" she employs accessible language, defining conceptual terms in everyday words.

Schecter pays attention to issues of race and class and their influence in both men's violent behaviour and women's experience. She is respectful in presenting the views of Black, Native Indian and other women of colour active in the shelter movement. She makes note of differences between middle class and poor and working class women, especially regarding external resources and internal resourcefulness commonly available to each. Perhaps most importantly, though, Schecter urges other activists to pay attention to differences of race, class, ethnicity, sexual orientation, etc. She argues that while it is both necessary and accurate to assert that battering crosses race and class lines, such assertions must not gloss over differences among women. She concludes this argument by saying: "Because the potential strength of the battered women's movement lies partly in its diversity, it is now at a point where in order to realize this potential, it must acknowledge the differences and struggle with them internally." Seven years after this book was published, Canadian transition houses and American shelters continue to struggle with these issues.

Ylló, Kersti & Michele Bograd, eds. *Feminist Perspectives on Wife Abuse.* Newbury Park: Sage, 1988. 318 pages, not indexed.

An interesting new anthology bringing together feminist activists, academics and counsellors. Because it is an anthology, and more particularly, because the writers have different groundings, the level of accessibility varies. The audience seems to be researchers--whether academic or not--but certainly front line workers will find the anthology useful, especially in its description of emerging issues and areas of study.

The text is divided into four parts. The first consists of three articles on the politics of research in wife abuse. The second, and for our purposes most important part, presents four examples of new feminist research. The third looks at clinical approaches to wife abuse, including treatment models for batterers and medical responses to battering. The last part explores some of the possibilities for collaboration between academics and activists.

In her introduction, editor Michele Bograd argues that while there is no single feminist perspective on wife abuse, all such perspectives have in common four elements or dimensions. First, they all look to concepts of gender and power as at least partial explanations for wife assault. Second, they all examine the family as an historical social institution. Third, feminist perspectives recognize the importance of understanding and validating women's experiences. Finally, feminist perspectives are dedicated to using scholarship for women.

In varying degrees these four elements are present in all of the articles in this book. Interestingly, the articles which, from our perspective and for our purposes, are the very best in the anthology are all versions of work published elsewhere and reviewed elsewhere in this Guide. Susan Schecter's article is a much condensed version of her book *Women and Male Violence,* annotated in this section of the Guide. Articles by Liz Kelly, Elizabeth Stanko and Dobash and Dobash all appear in *Women, Violence and Social Control*, edited by Jalna Hanmer and Mary Maynard and discussed in the last section of this Guide. Certainly there is nothing wrong (and much right) about versions of the same work appearing in different texts, but we will not repeat ourselves here.

Of the remaining articles in this anthology the most important for our purposes is a collaborative effort by Lee H. Bowker, Michelle Arbitell and J. Richard McFerron on the relationship of wife assault and child abuse. The authors say that among both professionals and lay people there is a common assumption that battered women abuse their children. To the contrary, the authors' research indicates that children of battered women are much more likely to be abused by their fathers. In fact, in their large sample the authors found "wife beaters abused children in 70% of the families in which children were present." This is an astonishing figure which, the authors point out, may be an underestimate. Given that it does not include child sexual abuse, neglect and many other categories of child abuse it certainly is an underestimate. The figure has important implications for those who work with battered women and battering men and the authors rightly suggest those workers should assume child abuse is present in at least 70% of the cases they deal with.

The drawback to this article is its academic language. Really, there is no need to use a term like "positive bivariate relation-

18

ship" when you want to say that domineering men are likely to hit their kids as well as their wives. Language aside, the article makes an important contribution both for front line workers in their immediate work and for all of us involved in long range efforts to trace and understand patterns of male violence. The same can be said of the anthology as a whole.

Other Useful Texts

Barnsley, Jan et al. *Battered and Blamed: A Report on Wife Assault from the Perspective of Battered Women.* Vancouver: Women's Research Centre with Vancouver Transition House, 1980. 141 pages, not indexed.

A qualitative study based on interviews with residents and workers at the former Vancouver Transition House. Very good description and analysis of women's experience of wife battering which is written in clear, accessible language.

Bishop, Joan. *Speaking Out: Voices of Battered Women in Cape Breton.* Sydney, N.S.: Cape Breton Transition House, 1988.

A series of papers, organized in a kit, including a statistical profile of transition house residents, women's descriptions of their experience in transition house, discussions of emotional abuse, and children of battered women. Like the above entry, largely a qualitative study in which the voices of battered women are heard.

Jones, Ann. *Women Who Kill.* New York: Fawcett Columbine, 1980. 422 pages, indexed.

In a chapter called "Totalling Women" Jones describes the experiences of battered women who finally kill their abusers. For each case she describes the history of the abuse, the circumstances of the killing, and the subsequent treatment of the woman in the courts and the media. Of course, most battered women do not kill their abusers; nevertheless, Jones' work provides important insights especially regarding differential attitudes toward men's and women's use of violence.

Picture: Dating Violence

Young women, in their teens and twenties, describe being beaten, sexually assaulted and verbally abused by their boyfriends. Sometimes their boyfriends just lost their tempers and slapped or pushed once. More often, though, the women say it didn't stop at one slap, that the attacks escalated to full-scale beatings. They describe how their boyfriends repeatedly punched them, kicked them, threw them against walls or down stairs, pulled out their hair, strangled them, beat them to unconsciousness. Many women were raped by their boyfriends. Their boyfriends didn't care that they hurt the women sexually; some boyfriends even were proud of the pain they inflicted, seeing vaginal and anal bleeding as proof of his maleness or telling the woman she was not "woman enough" if she could not take the pain of his sexual assaults. Some women describe being tied to a chair and raped and some describe gang rapes led by their boyfriends.

Some women say their boyfriends held guns at their heads or knives at their throats and threatened to kill them. Some say their boyfriends also threatened to kill the woman's family, especially her mother and sisters. Many women describe their boyfriends criticizing their appearance - telling the women they were ugly, fat or not dressed properly. Some women were told they were stupid or crazy by their boyfriends. And many say their boyfriends called them names like "slut" and "whore" and "bitch," questioning their sexual behaviour without foundation.

Young women say their boyfriends tried to control their actions and behaviour, telling them where they could go and what they could do. The women talk especially of being kept isolated, not permitted by their boyfriends to spend time with family and friends of their choosing and of being threatened, beaten, or made to feel guilty when they did. For some the effect of this isolation was to cut them off from the help they needed to break free of the abusers and to increase their feelings of shame and fear.

In describing the fear they felt, young women beaten by their boyfriends speak of the constancy of fear, of being afraid all the time, of waking up scared in the morning. They say that part of the reason they were always afraid is that they didn't know what to expect: they couldn't predict whether or when their boyfriends would beat them and so were constantly on guard and constantly afraid. Some say they were afraid they were going to die. Some say that even after ending the relationship they continued to fear the abusers.

In addition to fear young women speak of guilt as an emotional consequence of the abuse they suffered. Many blamed themselves for their boyfriends' attacks and say that when they asked themselves "why me" they became depressed and insecure, believing there was "something wrong" with them. Some describe how they felt "crazy" or suicidal. Many women came to believe what the abusers said about them--that they were stupid, fat, lazy or crazy. Some, suffering the effects of sexual assault, say they came to see themselves in "pornographic images."

Some young women carried their feelings of self-blame even after they got out of the abusive relationship. They say they think they were "stupid" to put up with their boyfriends' violence. A few go so far as to say they must now "atone" for allowing men to think they could hurt women.

In blaming themselves these young women refrain from blaming the abusers. Most say that the violence caused them to feel sorry for their boyfriends. This is especially true when the young woman knew of abuse her boyfriend had suffered as a child. As one woman put it: "Part of the problem is we know their background. Women feel so much for them, their pain, and know all the horrible things that have happened to them."

Despite the guilt and fear and shame they felt, or perhaps because of it, young women tried to put a halt to their boyfriends' violence. Some tried to change their own behaviour--trying to be nicer, trying harder to please him--to become what their boyfriends seemed to want. Some say they tried to avoid provoking the men. Some tried to avoid being alone with the abusers, in the hope that the presence of others would prevent their boyfriends from hitting them. Many women, though, say that the presence of others had no effect--their boyfriends beat them in front of others and those others did and said nothing.

Many women tried to end the violence by getting out of the relationship, but they encountered a number of obstacles. Their boyfriends tracked them down, threatened to kill the young women and their families if the women rejected them. And violence left these women with little sense of identity separate from their boyfriends, little self-respect to use in asserting themselves to get free of these violent men. For some, the only way out they could see was suicide so they tried that. Some turned to their families for help but too many say their families either didn't believe them or didn't come to their aid. Other women, though, did get help from their families. Similarly, of the young women who sought professional intervention from police, social workers, etc., some received active assistance while others were dismissed as "hysterical."

Unable to halt the violence, or not believing they had the right not to be beaten, young women found ways to endure their boyfriends' abuse. Some used alcohol. Others speak of distracting themselves--thinking of other things to avoid thinking about the abuse. And some describe methods of dissociation similar to those used by child sexual abuse victims: forgetting, numbing, and leaving the body as "it" was being assaulted.

From women's descriptions, it appears that young men who beat, sexually assault and verbally abuse their female partners expect of women what their wife-battering elders expect. Women say their abusive boyfriends wanted them to look sexually attractive by the men's standards. They say the men demanded that the women be submissive and obedient and that the men saw them as "only needing to serve him." Some women speak of their boyfriends' possessiveness: "he didn't want what he had but he didn't want anyone else to have it either." And, as commented on earlier, some women describe how their boyfriends used women's bodies as proof of maleness or virility. These men were angry when the women didn't get pregnant when the men wanted them to, and pleased with themselves when the woman bled from their sexual assaults.

When the young women didn't meet these expectations-- when they were "disobedient" or failed to demonstrate the proper degree of submissiveness--their boyfriends beat them. Some women say that something as simple as not wanting or liking what their boyfriends wanted--to go swimming, the food he ordered at a restaurant--was enough to bring on an attack. And, of course, many young women say that jealousy and accusations of infidelity were the "reasons" their boyfriends hit them.

Many young women say that their boyfriends apologized after beating them. Sometimes the men also promised never to do it again. It seems that to these young men, saying "I'm sorry" was enough to make their violence dismissible. Other young men blamed the women for the attacks, saying the women provoked the violence or, particularly in the case of sexual assault, that it was something the women wanted or needed. Finally, some women say their boyfriends blamed external factors--"school's getting to me"--or claimed to have no control over their actions.

Young women say that being beaten by their first or second serious boyfriend changes how they view men and relationships in general. Some say that while they were being abused they came to think that all relationships are abusive. They say they wondered if it gets any better and some, concluding that it doesn't, say they stayed in the relationship because "why bother starting a new one" which will also be abusive. A few say they turned to prostitution, seeing it as "a good way to be in relationships with men." Others say their experience convinced them that all men "automatically" think women are stupid. And some describe a legacy of fear that men in general will attack them.

The Texts

Mercer, Shirley Litch. *Not a Pretty Picture: An Exploratory Study of Violence Against Women in High School Dating Relationships.* **Toronto: Education Wife Assault, 1988. 35 pages, not indexed.**

The issue of dating violence, or girlfriend abuse--the physical, verbal, emotional and sexual abuse of young women by their male partners--is a subject to which little attention has been paid. Perhaps in part this is because teenage women seem "in between," no longer dependent children yet not quite adults. Additionally, adults tend to both romanticize and trivialize teenage relationships as innocent, not very serious "puppy love." Yet like their older sisters, teenage women are beaten, verbally abused and sexually assaulted by the men they love.

Shirley Mercer says that the motivation for this book came from young women themselves. Giving talks to high school students on wife assault, she was asked "Why don't you talk to us about our violent boyfriends?" Discovering virtually no literature on the subject, Mercer undertook this study. Though it is a preliminary investigation, it clearly indicates that for many young women, "puppy love" is a violent, debilitating experience.

It's difficult to discern Mercer's intended audience. Given the study's origin, one would assume it is teenage women yet Mercer's language and presentation are too academic to appeal to a general audience. This is unfortunate, for, as feminist experience in other issues of violence against women has shown, a critical first step in the journey from victim to survivor is learning "I'm not the only one."

Mercer certainly writes from a feminist perspective. In describing the context of her work she begins by stating that "the patriarchal structure and ideology of western society legitimizes men's acts of violence against women of any age." She then briefly discusses the socialization of both girls and boys to traditional gender roles and concludes that adolescence is a time when young people act out those roles "sometimes to their worst extremes."

In preparing this study Mercer surveyed a total of 304 young women and men attendant at metropolitan Toronto high schools. Of those, twenty per cent of the young women reported experiencing at least one form of abuse--physical, verbal, sexual--in a dating relationship. Interestingly, thirteen per cent of the young men reported having inflicted some form of abuse on a female partner--a surprisingly high figure given what we know from women's accounts that often men don't recognize or admit that their behaviour is abusive.

Mercer also asked the students about violence in their homes. Nearly half reported that physical assault had occurred in their homes and more than half reported verbal abuse. Mercer goes on to say: "No significant correlation was found to exist within this sample between violence in the home and violence in a dating relationship." She does not comment on this finding (or non-finding), which is unfortunate given Mercer's earlier statements on socialization, gender roles, and the legitimacy accorded to men's violence against women. For example, if as this finding suggests, young people don't learn violence in their homes, where do they learn it?

Mercer followed up her survey by interviewing some of the young women. She records how those young women describe their confusion at their boyfriends' abusive behaviour, their silence about the abuse and resulting isolation, and, sadly, their belief that even an abusive boyfriend is better than no boyfriend at all. They and their sisters deserve better. By listening to them, by naming the violence done to them by their male partners, Mercer has helped us all in taking the first step toward ending that violence.

Other Useful Texts

Flerchinger, Billie Jo & Jennifer J. Fay.
Top Secret: A Discussion Guide. **Santa
Cruz: Network Publications, 1985. 53 pages,
not indexed.**

Intended for teachers and other group leaders to facilitate
discussion using the booklet *Top Secret: Sexual Assault Information for Teenagers Only.* Covers acquaintance rape, incest,
sexual exploitation and rape by strangers. This is not meant to
be an analytical work but as a discussion guide it is very useful.

Kostash, Myrna. *No Kidding: Inside the
World of Teenage Girls.* **Toronto: McLel-
land & Stewart, 1987. 422 pages, not indexed.**

Has a discussion of dating violence, drawn in part from
research conducted by Battered Women's Support Services of
Vancouver. Unfortunately, the discussion is very short.

Picture: Child Sexual Abuse

In recounting how they were sexually abused as children, women describe a range of assaults from fondling to vaginal penetration by fingers, hands, objects and penises to outright sexual torture. Some were forced to masturbate the abusers' penises, some were held down as the abusers masturbated upon them. Some were penetrated anally and orally. Some were forced to look at pornography and to act it out for the abuser's pleasure. Some were beaten, strangled, called names like "whore" or threatened with death as they were being sexually abused. Some were impregnated; some suffered physical injuries ranging from urinary tract infections to massive tearing and scarring of internal organs.

These women say that as children they felt tremendous isolation which was associated with feeling different, guilty and ashamed. Isolation also made them feel fearful. Many describe fearing that they would be killed by the abusers. They also talk about the constancy of the fear and the unpredictability--never knowing whether or when the next attack would come--which added to their constant state of fear.

For some of these women the assaults began in infancy, when they had no power to act to avoid the abuse or even to speak their objections. Older children did try to stop the abuse but precisely because they were children--female children being acted upon by male adults--their options were limited and largely ineffective. Some tried to tell another adult either directly or indirectly in words, or in actions which were often self-destructive. Some tried to avoid the abusers, running away if necessary. Some, believing the abuse was a punishment, tried to be perfect. Some tried to tell the abusers to stop. Some tried to stop the abuse by removing the only actor they had power over--they tried to kill themselves.

Because these strategies were not successful these children sought ways to endure the abuse. Some distracted themselves by fantasizing or by simply not thinking their own thoughts. As adolescents and young adults some dulled their awareness of the pain with alcohol and drugs. Some dissociated from themselves by forgetting or blocking from memory what was being done to them; by numbing themselves and so cutting themselves off from their feelings; or by "leaving their bodies"--separating themselves from the "object" being acted upon.

The sexual abuse produced in these children profoundly negative thoughts and feelings about themselves. Women describe feeling guilty, blaming themselves for the abuse done to them, and hating themselves because of it. Many women say that as children they felt ugly, soiled, dirty. Some, trying to explain the abuse to themselves, came to believe that there was something wrong or evil about them. Virtually all speak of having felt deeply ashamed.

For many women the negative thoughts and feelings about themselves lasted well into adulthood. Some speak of feeling marked forever as a victim; some describe themselves as life-long prisoners; some say they have suffered irreparable damages. For many the explicitly sexual nature of the assaults left them with a distorted sense of their sexual beings in adulthood: they struggle with sadomasochistic fantasies (the learned linking of pain and pleasure, sexuality and violence) or see themselves as "sluts" for having sexual feelings at all.

In contrast to all this negativity directed toward themselves, women's descriptions of their thoughts and feelings about the abusers are mixed. Some say that as children they felt only anger and hate, wishing the abuser would die. Many sum up their feelings as "terror." Others, though, describe a feeling of compassion, of being protective of the abuser and of feeling responsible for his needs. As adults who are dealing with their childhood experiences of abuse, some women continue to hate and fear their abusers while others are more dismissive, seeing the abusers as incompetent, weak, or just twisted.

Being sexually abused by men in childhood significantly affects how adult women view men and relationships. Many conclude from their childhood experiences that all men are abusive--unthinking, unfeeling sexually violent animals. Some are convinced that because they were sexually abused as children, as adults they are easy targets for men's sexual violence, even that men have a kind of radar and can pick them out for abuse. Many describe feeling generally fearful of men as men.

And what of the men? What do they say about their sexual abuse of children? Some women report that after assaulting them the abusers apologized and promised it wouldn't happen again, though of course it did. Some women say the abusers blamed them for the assaults, claiming the victim was in control or that she was a whore and wanted to be raped. For other women the abuse was passed off as sex education. Still others say the abuser claimed the victim was "special": that she was the only one who could do what he needed, that what he did to her was their shared secret, or that it was a "relationship." Some abusers characterized it as just a fun little game between them. Some women say the abusers claimed not to be responsible for their actions, that they could only respond to the imperatives of their erect penises.

Finally, many women say the abusers gave no explanation. This suggests the most common reason a man sexually abuses a female child: his assumption that it is natural for him to get what he wants. As one woman put it, "because my father wanted to abuse me. That's why it happened."

Women's descriptions of what men seem to expect or require of the female children they sexually abuse correspond in many respects to what men in the other pictures seem to expect of women. One is that the child-victim look sexually attractive by the abuser's definition. Another is ownership or possession--an object owned by the abuser, with which he can do what he wants. Most horribly, some women describe how the abuser used the victim's body as proof of his maleness or virility.

For many children the sexual abuse is not a secret. Women describe the responses they received from the adults around them whom they told or who otherwise knew of the abuse. Some women say the adults didn't understand, either because the child didn't have the language to describe what was being done to her or because the child's "language" was actions which were not noticed, questioned or adequately interpreted. Some women say as children they were not believed, especially in the face of the abusers' denials. Some women describe a kind of tacit support for the abuser from adults who laughed and joked about his abusive behaviour. Finally and most devastatingly, some women describe how the discovery that one man was sexually abusing a child led another man to abuse her, as if her status as "damaged goods" gave him permission.

The Texts

Butler, Sandra. *Conspiracy of Silence: The Trauma of Incest.* San Francisco: New Glide Publications, 1978. 208 pages, not indexed.

An important early book which, though it has its drawbacks,

is still one of the most frequently cited texts on child sexual abuse. Its strength lies in its description. Butler says she interviewed "hundreds" of women and men, including survivors, their mothers, and offenders. Their stories, told in their own words, appear throughout the text.

In this book Butler only deals with what she calls "incestuous assault," which means she does not address sexual abuse of children outside the family. This is not necessarily a limitation for, as Butler points out, the vast majority of child sexual abuse offenders are adult men related to their victims--fathers, stepfathers, grandfathers.

Butler says that what constitutes incestuous assault is any sexual activity which results in "emotional, physical or sexual trauma." It may involve manual, oral, or genital contact or it may involve no physical contact at all, as in the example Butler cites of a man watching his daughter undress. It is important to remember that child sexual abuse involves a range of intrusive behaviours. Still, the stories the children tell are, for the most part, stories of acting and being acted upon sexually.

Butler says that only rarely do men use threats of physical force to coerce a child into performing sexually, for the simple reason that it isn't usually necessary. Rather, she says most children are exploited in subtle ways, beginning with the imbalances of power, decision-making ability and understanding which exist between adults and children. She argues that children, particularly girls, don't have the resources to halt the abusers' behaviour. All children are taught to respect adult authority and to do what they are told, but in addition, "young girls are trained to adapt themselves to male needs by behaving in non-aggressive, non-competitive, compliant and passive ways." Accordingly, Butler argues that in "acquiescing" to the abuse, the child is adapting to her environment in the only way she can.

Butler says that men who sexually abuse their daughters, like other men, are "conditioned to having their needs met by women." She argues that those men expect their wives to be passive, respectful, undemanding, willing to change their own activities to match the men's wishes, and always sexually available. When those expectations are not met the men substitute their daughters for their wives. If they are discovered, they offer various rationales--sex education, the child was provocative, the mother frigid--the purpose of which is to place "blame, guilt and responsibility outside themselves and their control."

Some of the young women and men interviewed for this book were involved in street prostitution and Butler does a good job in exploring the links between these issues. She says that for sexually abused children sex can be a survival skill, "a way to get what she or he needs." Prostitution, then, can be a "logical extension of selling sex at home." Or the child or young woman may decide that if she has to have sex with men she might as well get paid for it. Most interestingly, Butler speculates that some survivors enter prostitution in order to assure themselves that all men are abusive, and hence that their abusive fathers are simply like other men.

Butler is also good at exposing and debunking two common myths about child sexual abuse: the seductive child and mother-blaming. Both direct attention away from the offender's responsibility. She says little girls learn seductive behaviour from the adults around them. They are encouraged and rewarded for being cute and sexy. At the same time, though, girls are socialized to "internalize guilt for such learned behaviour." The result, says Butler, is that girls are "preprogrammed to blame themselves" when they are abused. That self-blame is reinforced by mental health professionals and the general public perpetuating the myth of the seductive child.

Butler's extensive discussion of mother-blaming, particularly among professionals, is summed up as follows:

> The two words which consistently intrude upon all theory and analysis concerning mothers . . . are "abandoning" and "colluding." These are the names of their crimes, the reasons they are held responsible for the actions of others.

Of course, it doesn't matter what these mothers do--taking a job to support the family or even giving birth to another child can be "proof" of the mother's guilt according to these theories.

For all its ground-breaking description and analysis, this book does have its drawbacks. For example, Butler at times uses neutral or gender inclusive terms to describe offenders, e.g., "adults" or "him or her." It is jarring to find women--whom Butler says make up only three per cent of all offenders--given equal status with men in this regard. Butler also sometimes seems to lose sight of the hierarchy of harm children suffer. For example, in discussing negative sexual attitudes that exist in most families--not just those in which children are sexually abused--Butler says that repression and denial of sexual feelings and curiosity can lead parents to inflict "the ultimate sexual violence upon [children]: the denial of their right to their own bodies--the right to learn about them, to touch and enjoy them, to share them when they choose and to live wholly and delightedly within them." To say that a child who is told not to ask questions about sexuality or to explore her body has suffered the "ultimate sexual violence" is both to equivocate the word violence and to make less visible the very real harm of children raped, sodomized, used in pornographic pictures by their fathers and other men.

Obviously, Butler does take the harm of child sexual abuse seriously, and her work remains one of the most important references in the field.

Martens, Tony, with Brenda Daily and Maggie Hodgson. *The Spirit Weeps: Characteristics and Dynamics of Incest and Child Sexual Abuse with a Native Perspective.* **Edmonton: Nechi Institute, 1988. 134 pages, not indexed.**

Until now the experiences of Canadian Native victims and survivors of child sexual abuse have gone largely unrecorded. Perhaps in part this is because most researchers are white and urban-based. Perhaps, too, it is because the issue has been kept hidden, even more so than in non-Native communities. Over the past few years, though, more and more information has surfaced on extensive, often multi-generational sexual abuse of Native children both in residential schools and in their home communities. This book is not explicitly feminist. To our knowledge, though, it is the first book to specifically address Native perspectives on child sexual abuse. As such, it is groundbreaking.

The book's subtitle is an accurate reflection of its contents. The first ten chapters, written by a clinician, provide a racially non-specific description of child sexual abuse, focussing on the "psychological characteristics" and "behavioural symptoms" of victims, offenders and other family members. To this rather clinical description is added a Native perspective: in the first ten chapters footnotes are added to "clarify some Native aspects" of the issues being discussed and the last two chapters speak directly to Native experience. It is these two chapters which make this book so important.

Brenda Daily describes the historical context within which child sexual abuse occurs in Native communities. She notes significant features of the history of contact with white society--the whiskey trade, residential schools, etc.--as well as native culture, heritage, spirituality and concept of the "Elder." She then briefly discusses characteristics of individuals in incestuous families specific to Native peoples and, at some greater length, looks at why child sexual abuse is so often denied among Native peoples.

Among the factors Daily identifies as contributing to denial, some are specific to Native communities. For example, loyalty to the community often results in a reluctance of victims to bring in white outsiders who, with good reason, are often seen as oppressors rather than helpers. Other factors Daily describes, while perhaps having greater influence among Native peoples, are also often present in non-Native families and communities. Daily comments, for example, that adult women who were sexually abused as children sometimes see the abuse as simply "a woman's lot," and therefore don't respond adequately when their own children are abused. Similarly, when the abuse occurs in several generations of the same family it can come to be accepted as "this is how it is."

In the last part of her chapter Daily looks at "dually affected families," those in which both substances and people are abused. Though alcoholism does not "cause" child sexual abuse it is often used as an excuse. Daily says an alcoholic will not necessarily stop sexually abusing when he stops drinking. She argues, though, that in dealing with the two abusive behaviours, the substance abuse must be addressed first. The same holds true for the victims and other family members who abuse substances: they must first gain sobriety before they can deal with the sexual abuse. This does not mean that Daily would ignore sexual abuse or allow it to continue while the substance abuse is being treated, for the very first step of her proposed programme for dually affected families is: "Separate the individuals and get everyone to safety."

In the final chapter of the book Maggie Hodgson explores how to develop effective child sexual abuse treatment programmes in Native communities. She begins by arguing that such programmes must be community-based, and then describes features of Native communities which can inhibit the effectiveness of such an approach.

Like Daily, Hodgson makes note of the high incidence of alcoholism in Native communities. Interestingly, she points to some recent experiences in Native communities which suggest that when those communities are successful in achieving a high rate of sobriety, the number of disclosures of child sexual abuse increases. Accordingly, she proposes that when communities are planning alcoholism programmes they should at the same time make plans to deal with increased reports of sexual abuse. Similarly, she says that multiple charges of sexual abuse in one community can lead to even more disclosures and these should be planned for.

The clinical description of child sexual abuse which forms the bulk of this book is not unique. It and the proposed treatment model derive from a clinical programme which, as the authors say, "operates in the white world." Like other clinical approaches, it tends toward a disease model and lacks social analysis. This leads to treatment goals which, in our opinion, are inappropriate in many cases of child sexual abuse, for example, "reconstructing the family" and "re-integrating the offender" into the family.

In her Foreword Brenda Daily says: "I think that Natives and non-Natives have a great deal to learn from one another, and there is no robbery in fair exchange." We agree there is nothing inherently wrong in adapting knowledge and expertise developed in the white world for use in Native communities. There is, though, a great need for more descriptions of Native experiences of child sexual abuse and of responses developed by Native communities themselves. This book, particularly the chapters by Daily and Hodgson, form a starting place. This book can make a contribution to stopping child sexual abuse among Native peoples, because it says the problem exists, that Native communities must take it seriously, and that it doesn't have to be a way of life.

Rush, Florence. *The Best Kept Secret: Sexual Abuse of Children.* **Englewood Cliffs: Prentice-Hall, 1980. 226 pages, indexed.**

This text is primarily an analysis of the historical, religious, political and social traditions of East Indian and Western cultures which permit and even celebrate the sexual abuse of children by men. As such it is more a social critique than a descriptive work, though Rush does begin with "A Look at the Problem," and throughout the text supports her analysis with testimonies of women survivors.

Rush's greatest strength is her direct and uncompromising language and analysis. She locates child sexual abuse within the social context of misogyny and male supremacy, especially "centuries of programming total populations in the belief of a man's right to exercise sexual power and privilege." She argues that men consider sexual access to children to be their right and that that right is reinforced throughout our history and culture. She points to the eroticization of children both in mainstream films and advertising and in pornography as encouraging and legitimizing men's sexual abuse of children. She also devotes a chapter to so-called sexual liberationists. Their endorsement of adult-child sex in the name of sexual freedom for children Rush describes as "a euphemism for sexual exploitation," a movement whose motivation is not child rights but adult gratification.

Another chapter examines the sexual abuse of boys. In it Rush argues that inasmuch as boy children are dependent and powerless, they share the feminine gender with girls and women and because of this are targets of men's sexual abuse. The difference comes, Rush argues, in how boys experience and interpret their sexual abuse. She says that while virtually all of the women she interviewed reported strongly negative reactions to their childhood sexual abuse, the men's responses ranged from anger and frustration to shame or humiliation, to ambivalence to pride and pleasure. Rush attributes this difference to the social valuation of male and female sexuality and status: "The male knows that one day his sexuality will signify strength and superiority whereas to the female, sex with a male adult emphasizes her traditional secondary status." Rush's argument is borne out to some extent by the examples she cites of male victims' distress at being treated as or taken for a woman. Rush is to be applauded for recognizing sexual abuse of boys as a distinct and important issue. Clearly, more investigation is needed into the similarities and differences between boys' and girls' experience.

In both her historical and her contemporary analyses of child sexual abuse Rush pays attention to the use of children in pornography and prostitution. She also makes passing reference to the mothers of child sexual abuse victims who are themselves abused by battering husbands and who therefore face even greater difficulties in protecting their children. And, as noted above, she locates child sexual abuse within the context of woman-hating and male privilege. In these discussions Rush does not directly address the contribution of child sexual abuse to the climate of terror that conditions women's lives, but certainly the connections are there.

Rush describes the trend among some researchers and therapists to attribute child sexual abuse to either the victim's or the mother's behaviour (or the offender's wife and/or mother) as evolving from "an ingrained attitude and time-proven successful strategy of blaming females for what men do." But diverting responsibility will not make the problem go away. To begin to address the issue of child sexual abuse Rush says we must first look at the elements of our culture which eroticize children and teach boys and men to hate women. Prior to that, though, is naming: "we must face and accept the fact that it is men, not women, who actually seduce, rape, castrate, feminize and infantilize our young, and it is time for them, rather than women, to be held responsible for destructive, exploitative sexual behaviour."

Sleeth, Pamela & Jan Barnsley. *Recollecting Our Lives: Women's Experience of Childhood Sexual Abuse.* **Vancouver: Press Gang Publishers, 1989, (forthcoming).**

This new book is valuable to feminists wanting to learn about women's experience of child sexual abuse and to counsellors assisting victims and survivors. Most importantly, though, it is valuable to mothers of children who have been sexually abused and to survivors themselves for making sense of their experience and discovering it is possible to break free from the consequences of childhood abuse.

In their Introduction the authors say: "All women's lives are touched by male violence." Those of us who were not sexually abused as children or beaten by our husbands or raped by friends or strangers know women who were. We all know men who have bought women's bodies. We've all encountered pornography in the corner grocery store. The list goes on and on. Sleeth and Barnsley argue that because male violence is pervasive, it defines women's lives: our physical boundaries, our sense of security on the street, at home and at work, our sexual practices whether we are lesbian or heterosexual. They conclude by saying that child sexual abuse survivors are not different from other women, that all of us struggle for autonomy and integrity in the face of the reality of male violence, and that accordingly, we can all learn from survivors' experiences.

The book is based on the stories of twenty-five women, some of them adult survivors, some of them mothers of children who were sexually abused. As the authors describe it, the book is an attempt to come to grips with the meaning of what those women say. In a sense, the book reads as a dialogue between those women and the authors, for the description and analysis are not separated but rather, play back and forth throughout the text.

It is an effective method of presentation, for in speaking *with* those women the authors both keep their own language accessible and ensure that each analytical step they take is firmly and demonstrably grounded in women's experience.

For this book the researchers interviewed mothers of children abused in recent years as well as adult survivors. This allows the authors to look at the generational differences in the experience of child sexual abuse. In the twenty or more years since the adult survivors were abused, some progress has been made in the common awareness of child sexual abuse and in the resources available both to victims and to their mothers. While probably as many children, if not more, are sexually abused today as were a generation ago, today's mothers are in a somewhat better position to discover the abuse, to stop it and protect their children from further abuse, and to find the help both they and their children need in recovering.

The onus for stopping the abuse still rests with women and their children. The mothers' descriptions of their efforts to get action from social welfare and civil and criminal justice systems are a grim indictment of state institutions and societal attitudes in general. Still, these mothers could and did act to protect their children, something the mothers of a generation ago generally couldn't do. The inclusion of both adult survivors and mothers in this book, then, not only offers different perspectives or experiences of the abuse itself, but demonstrates the hard-won progress that has been made, and so gives reason to hope for tomorrow's children.

Of the women interviewed, both survivors and mothers, only one is a woman of colour. Rightly, the authors comment on this in describing their methodology and clearly state that given the relative homogeneity of their informants' racial and ethnic heritage, they cannot make generalizations about all women's experience of child sexual abuse. In short, the authors' task is to present and discuss the stories of the women they interviewed and they don't go beyond that.

The survivors interviewed suffered a range of abuses. Some were "just" fondled; others were raped and sexually tortured. For some the abuse was a few isolated incidents; for others it was an almost daily fact of life for years. This range of experience of abuse means that the book has relevance to all survivors. It also allows the authors to affirm repeatedly that regardless of the specific nature of the assaults, the presence or absence of threats or physical violence, etc., "it all hurts and it all has consequences."

American feminist Sonia Johnson recently has written on the

importance of telling the truth. It's something all of us, including feminists, have trouble doing. We avoid speaking the words because they're hard to say and hard to hear. We seek safety in the neutral language of theory which distances both speaker and listener from the painful reality of women's lives. But when we stop telling the truth we lose our very foundation and, accordingly, our right to speak at all.

The truth about child sexual abuse is often horrifying, enraging, sickening, but that is precisely why it must be spoken. In one of the most powerful passages of the book Sleeth and Barnsley juxtapose women's descriptions of the "acts" of sexual abuse with the "consequences" the women and children suffered. To every male apologist who, in ignorance or deceit, has ever argued that child sexual abuse is harmless, this passage gives chilling answer.

A significant analytical innovation of this book is what is called the "Survivor's Cycle." It depicts what the authors consider to be the sequence of internal experience and beliefs common to child sexual abuse victims. While some readers may take issue with the order and configuration of the cycle--indeed, its very circularity may be problematic--its value lies in its ability to make sense of a host of disparate psychological processes, feelings, beliefs and behaviours. For survivors it explains why twenty or thirty or forty years after the fact they are still suffering the consequences of what was done to them as children. Most importantly, though, Sleeth and Barnsley use the cycle to explain how survivors can come to live free of those consequences. In what they call "Exits from the Cycle," they first describe the steps the mothers took in stopping the abuse and protecting their children. They then describe the adult survivors' process of naming what was done to them, understanding what that meant, appreciating the skills they developed in order to survive, and regaining, or gaining for the first time, a sense of themselves as whole, worthy, good people.

The stories of the survivors and mothers in this book are stories of soul-destroying sexual, physical and emotional assault. They are also, though, stories of strength and courage, of the power of survival. In presenting these stories, in telling the truth about child sexual abuse in a clear and rigorous feminist voice, Sleeth and Barnsley help us all to better understand the reality of male violence and women's ability to live beyond it.

Other Useful Texts

Bass, Ellen & Laura Davis. *The Courage to Heal: A Guide for Women Survivors of Child Sexual Abuse.* **New York: Harper and Row, 1988. 491 pages, indexed.**

There are now a number of "recovery" or "healing" books available for child sexual abuse survivors. This is one of the best. It is designed as a workbook but can also be read on its own. The survivors' stories, called "Courageous Women," and the authors' discussion of the issues involved in recovering, are valuable in and of themselves. Recommended for survivors, their supporters, and for counsellors.

Bass, Ellen & Louise Thorton, eds. *I Never Told Anyone: Writings by Women Survivors of Child Sexual Abuse.* **New York: Harper & Row, 1983. 278 pages, not indexed.**

A collection of first person accounts, written by survivors. Some are well known and have been published previously, e.g, Maya Angelou's *I Know Why the Caged Bird Sings.* Others were written specifically for this anthology. The collection is organized according to the offender's relationship to the victim: father, friend, stranger, etc. The accounts express pain, confusion, horror, betrayal but also great courage and healing. Introductory essays by the two editors and Florence Rush help to place both the abuse and the healing into context.

Danica, Elly. *Don't: A Woman's Word.* **Charlottetown, P.E.I.: gynergy books, 1988. 94 pages.**

A powerful, often horrifying first person account, written in an almost stream-of-consciousness form. In the Introduction Nicole Brossard describes it as "the story of a heroine," and indeed, Danica's process of remembering and recording is an epic, heroic journey. Readers can expect to feel rage, horror, dismay but also awe.

**Mitchell, Alanna. "Child Sexual Assault,"
in Connie Guberman & Margie Wolfe, eds.,
*No Safe Place: Violence Against Women
and Children*. Toronto: Women's Press,
1985, pp.85-108.**

A good and concise introduction to child sexual abuse. Mitchell neatly reviews available statistical information, debunks common myths--especially the seductive child and mother blaming--and supports her description of the child's experience with quotes from adult survivors. She pays attention to the similarities and differences between boys' and girls' experience and describes the ongoing victimization of the girls as adults. Her attitude toward legislative reform (the article was written prior to the 1988 Criminal Code amendments) is refreshing: "The main reason to change the laws . . . is to send more offenders to jail," the point being not so much punishment or rehabilitation for offenders as protection for our children.

**Stanko, Elizabeth. "Incest: Some of Us
Learn as Children," in *Intimate Intrusions:
Women's Experience of Male Violence*.
London: Routledge & Kegan Paul, 1985. 14
pages.**

Though too short to stand on its own as a description, this is a very good and readable analysis of child sexual abuse as a form of men's violence against women. See full review in the last section of this Guide.

Picture: Workplace Sexual Harassment

When women recount their experiences of sexual harassment in the workplace they describe a range of insulting, intimidating and threatening actions by male co-workers, supervisors and clients. Many women say the men they work with display pornographic pictures and pictures of nude women in common work areas. Others describe male co-workers and supervisors aggressively staring at them or "addressing our breasts" when speaking to women. Verbal abuse, particularly of a sexual nature, is a common experience for working women. Women describe men making derogatory remarks about their appearance--calling a woman "Turtle Tits," for example. Others describe men telling dirty jokes to or in front of women, describing their sexual fantasies and making sexual remarks to and about the women: "God, I'm horny" or "I would love to get in the sack with you." Other women describe men asking or speculating about their sexual behaviour and orientation. And many women say the men they work with make abusive comments about women's intelligence and competence. They say these comments may be directed at an individual woman or women in general.

Some women say the sexual harassment they have suffered includes physical assault. Some describe men apparently accidentally touching them--brushing or squeezing up against their bodies, touching their breasts. Others describe more blatant contact. They say their male co-workers and supervisors slap their bottoms, put things down their blouses, poke and pat "any place they see fit to touch," hug and kiss the women. Some women describe being cornered in elevators, stairwells, storerooms and being held, their arms pinned, while the man touched and kissed the woman. The women say these assaults were sometimes accompanied by threats to rape.

Many women say their supervisors told them, directly or by implication, that they had to "play along" with the men's sexual advances in order to receive job benefits or even to avoid being fired. Some say they were given dirty tasks or stricter supervision because they were not "nice enough" to their supervisors and refused to date them. A few were told outright that they had to trade sex for something as simple as a requested night off. For many women, particularly young women just entering the workforce, the men's words were backed up: when they didn't "play along," when they refused a date or objected to their supervisors pawing them, they were fired.

In describing their reactions to being sexually harassed women say they felt embarrassed, degraded and humiliated. Some say they felt ashamed to tell anyone about the harassment; a few say they felt guilty. Women who were repeatedly told they were stupid say they came to believe it and that both their work and their self-esteem suffered as a result. Much more than other victims of male violence, sexually harassed women say they felt angry. For many that anger was coupled with feeling frustrated, inadequate and powerless to change or prevent the men's harassment. Powerlessness also played a part in feeling afraid. Not knowing how to stop the men's harassment and being unable to predict what would come next left many women feeling physically afraid and afraid of losing their jobs.

Some women say they changed their own behaviour in order to try to stop the abuse. For some that meant changing how they dressed, for example, wearing aprons to hide their breasts. Many say they tried to avoid the individual men who were harassing them. Some confronted the harasser, though that often did not have the desired effect--some women say the harassment increased and others were fired. Some women took the issue to their union or to management. Of these some received a degree of support but many others say their complaint was "treated as a big joke" or that they were fired for being trouble-makers. Some talked to their female co-workers and received at least sympathy and validation.

The most effective strategy for stopping the abuse women describe, however, is to quit their jobs. Resigning is effective in stopping specific incidents of sexual harassment, though it does not guarantee it won't be repeated in the next workplace, and has serious consequences for the women's self-esteem and, of course, their economic well-being. When no action, even quitting, seemed possible, women kept quiet and tried to bear the sexual comments and leers and pawing in silence. In some cases they tried to pretend nothing had happened.

From women's descriptions it appears that men who sexually harass their female co-workers and subordinates see nothing wrong in their behaviour, that it is somehow their inalienable right, or that having entered the workplace, women are simply "fair game." It seems that these men expect women to be silent and compliant--to be "good sports," not complain of the men's harassment, tolerate their offensive pictures and comments, endure their physical assaults, comply with their sexual demands--or lose their jobs.

The Texts

Backhouse, Constance & Leah Cohen. *The Secret Oppression: Sexual Harassment of Working Women.* **Toronto: MacMillan, 1978. 208 pages, not indexed.**

Published more than ten years ago, this book is still considered the authoritative text on sexual harassment in Canada. The authors' description of the issue is based on first person accounts and their analysis is unapologetically feminist. While the language is not "plain English," it is readable.

In identifying the perpetrators of sexual harassment Backhouse and Cohen list bosses, supervisors, co-workers, clients and customers. What they have in common is that they are men and that they can create "job-related reprisals for a female worker who refuses [their] sexual advances." Backhouse and Cohen argue that these men are not sick or even just immature--they are men like other men, normal men. Like all men they have been taught to equate male sexuality with "power, virility, strength and domination." The authors say that far from being punished for sexual aggression against women, men are encouraged and applauded by other men. They also say that men do not see sexual harassment as offensive to women, noting that even among men who had been publicly exposed they were unable to find a single one who admitted to being a harasser.

Backhouse and Cohen contend that sexual harassment is "one of the most compelling problems confronting women in society." Without getting into a debate about who is the greatest victim, this does seem something of an overstatement. The authors are correct, though, in locating workplace sexual harassment at a crossroads, "encompassing both economic coercion and an aspect of violence against women."

In describing women's experience of sexual harassment Backhouse and Cohen state clearly that most women do not feel flattered. They say that for most women the experience generates fear, anxiety and anger leading to impaired job performance, depression and sometimes physical ailments such as hypertension. Backhouse and Cohen also say that women often blame themselves for men's harassing behaviour, especially because as women they are socialized "to think that it is their responsibility to control sexual matters."

While they make a point of noting that middle class and professional women suffer sexual harassment as much as lower class women, Backhouse and Cohen do not comment on the experiences and particular vulnerability of immigrant women and women of colour. It seems to us that sexual and racial harassment often are linked. Additionally, farm workers, domestic workers and others have said that immigrant women often don't know their employment rights, fear deportation if they draw attention to themselves and, accordingly, are often targetted for exploitation, including sexual harassment.

In what is, from our perspective, one of the most important passages of the book, Backhouse and Cohen discuss sexual harassment's link with violence against women in general and rape in particular. They describe how violence against women has been tolerated and even encouraged in our culture and society, noting that sexual access to women and physical domination are considered "male prerogatives." They say that inasmuch as sexual harassment is one of the more subtle forms of violence against women it is not surprising that it is a "secret oppression." More specifically, they say that seeing the derision with which rape victims and battered wives are treated, sexually harassed women are unlikely to speak out about their own victimization. The argument is an important one, for it indicates the ideological and experiential commonality among issues of violence against women.

The weakest section of this book concerns solutions to the problem. While the authors re-state that sexual harassment is not a personal problem of individual women, they nevertheless suggest personal prevention tactics which are at best questionable, such as dressing "unspectacularly." Similarly, their proposed action plan for management seems naive, especially given their own finding that most management personnel do not acknowledge sexual harassment exists or is a serious problem.

Their discussions of union plans and possible legislative changes are better though now perhaps somewhat dated.

In sum, this book is a good beginning discussion of workplace sexual harassment. Now, more than ten years since the book's publication, that discussion should be developed upon further.

MacKinnon, Catharine A. *Sexual Harassment of Working Women.* **New Haven: Yale University Press, 1979. 312 pages, indexed.**

This is an awesome/awful book. Awesome because MacKinnon's depth and clarity and grace of thinking are breath-taking, and awful because, in spite of her stated desire to speak to both a legal and a general audience, MacKinnon's language is frustratingly and often unnecessarily dense and formalistic. The book is also very American, in the sense of being rooted in and speaking to the specifically American legal, social and political experience and tradition. For all feminists, though, lawyers or not, American or not, the book makes an important contribution to our understanding of the system of male violence against women and the place of sexual harassment in that system.

MacKinnon pays attention to women's descriptions of their experience of sexual harassment, quoting extensively from first person accounts in one chapter in particular. Interestingly, she argues that "women's feelings about their experiences of sexual harassment are a significant part of its social impact," and that those feelings are a "material reality." In other words, she argues that women's feelings--anger, humiliation, powerlessness, degradation, fear, embarrassment--make a difference to real things in the world. In particular, MacKinnon maintains that women's feelings are part of the substance of the issue of sexual harassment, not extraneous to it, and hence must be taken into account when treating sexual harassment as a social issue.

MacKinnon also pays attention to the influence of race on women's experience of sexual harassment. In discussing the sexual harassment of black women by white men she says "sexual harassment can be both a sexist way to express racism and a racist way to express sexism." She also mentions sexual harassment of black women by black men and of white women by black men. She concludes, though, that "although racism is deeply involved in sexual harassment, the element common to these incidents is that the perpetrators are male, the victims female."

This statement of fact--that men are the abusers, women the victims--is the cornerstone of MacKinnon's analysis of all issues of violence against women. She argues that gender is a power division: men because they are men have power over women because they are women. What distinguishes MacKinnon's argument from those of other feminists is the emphasis she places on sexuality as one "sphere of expression" of that power division. In particular, she argues that in depicting issues such as rape as crimes of violence, not sex, feminists ignore the extent to which social conceptions of sexuality are shaped by gender inequality. In cases of sexual harassment she says it may be the very fact of women's vulnerability that arouses male sexual desire: "men feel they can take advantage, so they want to, so they do." According to this formulation, sexual harassment is normal male sexual behaviour, in which case, MacKinnon asks, how can it be treated as illegal?

MacKinnon's answer is sex discrimination law. Women are sexually harassed in the workplace because they are women and therefore economically and sexually subordinate to men. It is just such disparities of social power between classes of persons that discrimination laws are meant to address. At the time of writing this argument had little applicability to Canadian women. Since the Charter of Rights and Freedoms has been proclaimed, though, perhaps Canadian feminists should dust off their copies of this book to use in developing strategies to fight workplace sexual harassment. More generally, all feminists concerned with developing an analytical framework for understanding male violence can benefit from this early exploration of the relationships of sexuality, gender, power and violence. (MacKinnon's later work is discussed in the last section of this Guide)

Other Useful Texts

Graheme, Kamini Maraj. "Sexual Harassment," in *No Safe Place: Violence Against Women and Children*, edited by Connie Guberman and Margie Wolfe. Toronto: Women's Press, 1985, pp.111-130.

Graheme discusses sexual harassment in the workplace, in

academic settings, and on the street. More of a theoretical framing than a description of women's experience, the article looks at different definitions of sexual harassment and, more importantly, gives arguments for seeing sexual harassment as both a form of violence against women and a form of social control.

Robichaud, Bonnie. *A Guide to Fighting Workplace Sexual Harassment/Assault.* **Osgood: Bonnie Robichaud, 1988. 25 pages, not indexed.**

Bonnie Robichaud took her own complaint of sexual harassment to the Supreme Court of Canada and won. In the process she learned a lot about the various players--unions, human rights commissions, etc. Though intended for Ontario residents, this booklet is useful for any Canadian woman considering pursuing a sexual harassment complaint.

Picture: Rape/Sexual Assault

From rape crisis workers, with a range of experience in different centres over many years, we learned the following about women's experience of sexual assault:

A woman who is raped can be any woman. She may be the wife or co-worker of her attacker, she may be a prostitute raped by a trick. Most women are raped by men they know but some are raped by strangers. Rape victims can be any age and any class. What they have in common is their female gender and thus their vulnerability to male violence. That vulnerability takes different forms, for example, extreme youth or age makes women particularly vulnerable. And, the workers say, women have various ways of compensating for their vulnerability, modifying their lives to avoid being raped by, for example, not walking alone at night. But because the problem is not who women are but who men are, compensating doesn't always work.

What rape crisis workers call a "standard" rape is coercion that leads to penis/vagina penetration against the woman's will. That coercion can take the form of job threats or pressure to "come across" on a date. It needn't be overt: when the power imbalance between the man and the woman is magnified--teacher-student, doctor-patient--so-called "authority rape" happens.

But, the workers say, many rapes are not "standard." They say very often women are forced to perform sexually upon the rapist--fellatio, forced kissing, "hand jerking." They say women are beaten, tied up with phone cords, wire, pantyhose and some have brooms, hammers, broken bottles, dirt shoved in their anuses, vaginas, mouths. In some cases the rapist uses guns or knives. Some women are assaulted by more than one man at a time.

The workers say that as a man is raping a woman he will often verbally abuse her: call her whore, slut, douche bag, bitch, cunt.

He will often threaten to kill the woman, to kill her kids, or to make them watch as he rapes her. Overall, whether or not the men threaten, the workers say women believe they might be killed.

The workers say women have a kind of radar or "seventh sense" about the men who eventually rape them. They report that after the fact women say things like "I knew there was something about him," or "It crossed my mind . . . " Too often, though, women don't trust their radar, telling themselves "he doesn't look like a rapist." Or they don't act on it because to do so they would have to say no, be not nice, be assertive, transgress social norms, and so risk being called a bitch or a prude.

So the woman goes along with whatever it is the man has suggested. The workers say there then comes a "moment" when the woman realizes that something is going to happen to her and that what she wants no longer matters, that the man has breached her trust and taken control.

When the assault begins, the workers say, women try many things to stop it. What they try depends in part on the situation and their relationship to their attacker. A woman may scream, run, try to escape or reach help. She may beg, lie, or try to throw up to turn the man off. She may fight. She may try to talk or joke the man out of the attack, try to "hook the man into some sense of humanity." She may become totally passive, especially if the man is or threatens to be physically violent, hoping to avoid worse hurt and hoping that the sooner he is finished the sooner he will leave.

The workers say that what women think about most while they are being sexually assaulted is surviving: "I have to get through this." In enduring the assault they will use whatever coping skills they have developed. For some women, particularly those who have been abused before, coping means separating themselves, "This isn't happening to me," even dissociating as child sexual abuse victims do. Many women experience physical and psychological shock, and so are "numbed out." Depending upon their sense of knowledge and authenticity, the women may describe their experience as "Like watching a movie." Depending upon the situation, they may be distracted from what is being done to them by, for example, worrying about their kids in the next room.

The workers say that after being raped women move back and forth among the three stages of grief: denial, anger and acceptance. They say the process can take years and that sometimes women get stuck in denial: mind-blocking, denying that what was done to them was rape, or asserting "Life goes on,

I'm fine." Sometimes women will blame themselves, not for the rapist's behaviour, but for getting into the situation, for not paying attention to their radar. After being raped women commonly describe feeling powerless, sad, humiliated, not worthy, degraded, violated, ashamed, used. They describe a sense of loss, "like a piece of your soul or body has been taken away and will never be replaced." If a woman has been abused before, the recent assault validates what that experience taught her. In particular, if the woman was sexually abused as a child, she may feel marked as a victim. Yet, even women who have not suffered previous abuse will often say that simply because they are women, they are not surprised they were sexually assaulted.

The workers say that in recent years the overall "tenor" of response women get when they tell people they've been raped has changed for the better. In particular, they note that women often respond with "I was too." Husbands and boyfriends commonly respond with "I'm going to kill that bastard" but sometimes don't understand why three weeks or more after the rape the woman isn't "over it." The workers say responses from institutional personnel such as police are typified by "male officiousness" made worse by perceptions or prejudices, e.g., if the woman was drinking, dressed in a certain way, or is involved in prostitution she is less likely to be believed. The workers also say that the closer the relationship between the woman and her attacker the less likely it is she will be believed either by friends or by officials. Friends and co-workers may find it difficult to believe that someone they know is a rapist while officials may look at the relationship only, not at the rape.

Often, the workers say, a woman's feeling of vulnerability is magnified after she is raped: "the volume of fear that's there in every woman's life gets cranked up." For a time that fear may be generalized so the woman feels wary of all men and in all circumstances. Depending upon who her attacker was and what the circumstances were, a woman may feel fearful of particular categories of men, e.g., all men who are drunk or all men of one racial origin. The workers say that most women who have been raped try very hard not to hate all men, that they hope not all men are "like that." Nevertheless, women "look at men differently" after experiencing sexual assault. Their radar is reinforced and their level of trust goes down.

How rape victims look at men in general depends in part on how they explain to themselves what happened to them. Indeed, the workers say that that explanation is important for recovery, for how a woman survives. They describe three paradigms or systems of explanation: the feminist, the sociomedical, and the religious. The second is especially common: the workers say that because women can't believe that male violence is random, they explain their own rapes by saying the rapist is "sick" or had to "release."

The workers also say many women feel hatred toward the man who raped them; they may express a desire to kill and they are surprised and ashamed of feeling that way: "I know this sounds awful but I want to kill him."

Of the men who rape the workers say first that they plan their assaults. If weapons are involved the men select them beforehand. Just as women have a radar so do men--the men select their victims on the basis of who is least likely or able to enforce her personal boundaries. The workers say men who rape expect women to conform to a male definition of women's sexuality and that definition is based on men's demands. Rapists expect women to give in to men's demands and if women don't, the men will just take what they want as if it is their right. Sometimes the men will try to excuse their behaviour, either by blaming the victim--"you wanted it/asked for it/wanted me"--or by claiming not to have control--"I can't help it/I have uncontrollable urges." From the workers' perspective, for men power is wound up with sexuality such that power is male. When a man rapes a woman he feels more powerful than he ordinarily does, and therefore feels more male. This linking of sexuality and power is most explicit when sexual degradation becomes "experimentation with a thing," the "experimentation" being sexual torture, the "thing" being a woman's body.

The Texts

Brownmiller, Susan. *Against Our Will: Men, Women and Rape.* **New York: Simon and Schuster, 1975. 472 pages, indexed.**

Some books change the world. This is one of them. When it was published in 1975, it not only validated the experience of millions of rape victims, not only gave credibility to the women struggling to establish rape crisis centres, it changed the way all of us talk about sexual assault, and about the relations of men and women in general. Nearly fifteen years later, it is still a book women describe as changing their lives.

The book is a massive study. Among other things, it covers the legal history of rape as property theft, the place of rape in war, pogroms and slavery, the influence of race in rape, rapists and victims as popularly depicted and in reality, and rape in institutions, both prisons and the family. Women's descriptions of their experience are presented in one chapter as "testimonies" and are used to give meaning to statistics and to support Brownmiller's analysis of the reality of rape. Despite the book's length Brownmiller's language remains fresh and non-academic throughout.

What makes this book so important is Brownmiller's clearly articulated and well-argued feminist social analysis. In what is probably the most oft-quoted line of the book Brownmiller describes rape as "nothing more or less than a conscious process of intimidation by which all men keep all women in a state of fear." In a sense, the line sums up much of Brownmiller's analysis. She argues that all men, whether or not they actually rape, subscribe to a "male ideology of rape," which presents sexuality as conquest. She also says that rape is a planned and deliberate act of violence whose object is not sexual gratification but domination, possession and intimidation. Brownmiller concludes that because of the ever-present danger of rape, all women--victims and potential victims--fear all men--rapists and potential rapists.

Brownmiller speculates that rape originated somewhere in prehistory when men discovered that they have the equipment, so to speak; that their genitalia could be used as weapons to generate fear and that women cannot retaliate in kind. She says: "When men discovered that they could rape, they proceeded to do it." Brownmiller goes on to argue that prehistoric men's discovery of this accident of anatomy led to the most important and enduring forms of social organization: monogamy and the subjugation of women by men. From these developed the concepts of hierarchy, slavery and private property.

The argument is fascinating, highly speculative and, of course, unprovable. Its value is that it serves to shift the ground of one's thinking. It underscores that rape is an ordinary act performed by ordinary men who are supported in their sexual violence by other ordinary men. The argument does, though, lead the reader to a rather disturbing speculation on the future: if men rape simply or fundamentally because they are physically able to rape, and the fact of rape is what conditions our social organization, then what hope is there for a fundamental change in the relations of men and women?

Skipping ahead a number of centuries, Brownmiller argues that in the modern world "women are trained to be rape victims." She discusses at length the role of cultural artifacts--everything from fairy tales and comic books to confession magazines, television and pornography--in teaching women they are both a target of and responsible for men's sexual violence. Those same cultural artifacts teach men that more than just being their "right," sexual aggression against women is part of what being a man is.

Brownmiller locates child sexual abuse within the same ideological framework as the rape of adult women. Writing in 1975, prior to the publication of the most important feminist texts on the issue, she details some of what was then known of the incidence, experience and consequences of child sexual abuse, as well as its links with prostitution. She condemns the "unholy silence that shrouds" the issue and argues that that silence is "rooted in the same patriarchal philosophy of sexual private property that shaped and determined historic male attitudes toward rape."

Brownmiller also links sexual harassment and, more especially, pornography and prostitution to the male ideology and practice of rape. All three declare and celebrate men's supposed right to sexual access to women. They dehumanize women and encourage men to direct sexual hostility against women. Brownmiller argues that "the case against pornography and the case against toleration of prostitution are central to the fight against rape," because until these issues are confronted, "the false perception of sexual access as an adjunct of male power and privilege will continue to fuel the rapist mentality."

This is not an easy book to read. It is long, cross-cultural, pan-historical, and unrelenting in its analysis of the sexual horror men do to women. Some of its arguments are now considered if not dated then at least incomplete, and in the years since its publication other feminists have refined, and in some cases, rejected them. But Brownmiller's work remains our base--the boldest and clearest articulation of feminists' understanding of the place of rape in the lives and psyches of both women and men.

Clark, Lorenne & Debra Lewis. *Rape: The Price of Coercive Sexuality.* **Toronto: Women's Press, 1977. 222 pages, not indexed.**

This is the most important, and certainly most often cited Canadian study on rape. It does not have what we normally consider a grounded analysis, i.e., the analysis does not derive from first person accounts, but both the information and the analysis have made significant contributions to feminists' understanding of this issue.

Data for the study was obtained from files held by the Metropolitan Toronto Police Department. Clark and Lewis examined all cases of rape reported in one year and from that examination developed statistical profiles of the victims, perpetrators, and the crime itself. These profiles give a picture of some--but certainly not all--common experiences of rape and its aftermath. Because the data was derived from police reports following the Criminal Code provisions operable at the time, the study does not include the experiences of wives raped by their husbands, victims under the age of fourteen, and cases of sexual assault categorized as attempted rape or indecent assault. And, of course, the study does not include sexual assaults which were not reported to the police.

More than looking at the actors and the event of rape, Clark and Lewis examine how those are perceived, especially by police personnel. Of the 116 rapes reported, Clark and Lewis say the police classified 74 as "unfounded," whereas the authors considered only twelve unfounded. In explaining this disparity Clark and Lewis conclude that "to a very large extent, it is the character of the reporting rape victim which determines whether or not a reported offense will be classified as founded, and passed on in the judicial system." Women who were drunk, on welfare, separated, divorced or living common law, women with any history of psychiatric treatment are seen as women who "can't be raped." This does not mean that the police deny that an assault took place; only that those women are seen as having lost or forsaken their social value as women. Hence, in the police view, they do not make credible witnesses in the male dominated criminal justice system.

In a later chapter Clark and Lewis describe these women as "open territory victims." Rapists can attack them with impunity, for the only blame attached will be to the victim. Such victims are "women with an already diminished sexual and reproductive value, or women who have forfeited this value by defying traditional expectations of respectable, acceptable, female behaviour." For them there is no protection.

The perceptions of, and treatment received by, open territory victims are illustrative of a fundamental anti-woman bias in our society and institutions. In the second part of this book Clark and Lewis bring to bear a feminist analysis of that bias and the place of rape within it. Like Brownmiller and others, they look at the history of rape as a property offense. They argue that women are seen as "trustees" of their sexual and reproductive capacities, responsible for protecting those assets for their rightful male owner--first father then husband. Accordingly, Clark and Lewis say a woman who is raped is considered to have failed in this duty. She has taken unreasonable risks with someone else's property. Even if the risk is simply being in the world, she is responsible for it and for what happens to her.

Clark and Lewis contend that because sexual and reproductive capacities are seen as commodities, the best a woman can do is barter her body for the security and protection of marriage. She must advertise her goods while protecting them from handling. This means that from the perspective of men, women are "the hoarders and miserly dispensers of a much desired commodity, and men must constantly wheedle, bargain, and pay a price for what they want." The authors argue that this dynamic is the root of misogyny, for men resent having to pay for what they believe women should give them freely. This leads, say the authors, to a form of human sexuality which is fundamentally coercive, as men try to "bargain women down."

In the range of coercive bargaining methods men have at their disposal--persuasion, economic inducement, etc.--the threat or use of physical force is simply at the far end of a continuum. As such it is normal male behaviour, and Clark and Lewis argue persuasively that rapists are indeed normal men. Furthermore, they say that men see nothing abnormal in wanting to have sex with an unwilling partner because "they fear that if full, consensual sexuality were to become the standard of acceptable sexual relations, they would be deprived of many--perhaps most--of the sexual acts that they now enjoy."

The prescriptions for change Clark and Lewis advocate are largely tied to the old Criminal Code provisions. As those provisions have now been superceded--by legislation similar in some respects to what the authors propose--the specific recommendations are no longer applicable. Their background discussions of consent, coercion and assault, though, are still valuable. They tread on dangerous ground, however, when they move from the specific to the general. Clark and Lewis rightly argue that rape exists because women are not considered sexually and reproductively autonomous persons, and that only by dealing with that larger issue will rape cease to be a problem. They go on to say:

> It would be both unreasonable and unrealistic to prohibit all forms of coercive sexuality while any vestige remains of the old structures and their atten-

dant ideology. So long as men must bargain for sex,
it would be unjust to prohibit all coercive strategies.
But clearly there must be limits, and those limits
must be agreed upon by both men and women.

But how much more "unjust" is it to expose women to men's
coercive strategies, and, through silence, condone them? Furthermore, given men's sexual, political, economic and social
power over women how realistic is it to suppose that limits on
men's behaviour can be agreed upon? This passage suggests
that in the end the authors shy away from their own feminist
analysis. It is that analysis, cogently presented, that makes this
book still the best in Canada on the everyday experience of rape.

Russell, Diana E.H. *The Politics of Rape: The Victim's Perspective.* New York: Stein & Day, 1975. 311 pages, not indexed.

Diana Russell has written extensively on men's violence
against women and children. She has a number of full-length
books to her credit, all of them grounded in women's experience.
This one, though one of her earlier works, is the least academic.
It is also one of the best descriptions of rape available.
The bulk of the book consists of twenty-two first person accounts, presented as verbatim transcripts of interviews. Five of
these accounts address issues of race and racism. To each
account Russell adds commentary drawing out the analytical
issues each illustrates. The accounts show not only the various
circumstances under which women may be raped, they describe
who the men are, what they do to women, and most importantly,
how the women think and feel about their experience. Even
without Russell's commentary these accounts are invaluable.
Two accounts stand out as particularly illustrative of the
recurring pattern of male sexual violence in women's lives. In
the first a little girl of four was brutally raped by two young men.
From ages fourteen to seventeen the child was repeatedly
sexually abused by her step-father, who, in response to her
tears, said "Well, what difference does it make? You've had all
this before. Why should it bother you?" From ages seventeen
to almost twenty-three this same young woman was married to
a man who many times painfully raped her. The husband knew
of the woman's prior assaults and, though he didn't comment on
them directly, the woman wonders "whether the idea that he
could take me against my will was OK to him since it had already

happened."

At the conclusion of this woman's story Russell takes issue with the psychologists and others who claim that women who suffer many instances of abuse are "victim-prone," masochistic or in some way collaborate in their victimization. To the contrary she says that this story points to the view that "given one victimization, a person is more likely to experience further victimizations, because the very fact of having been victimized provokes aggressors."

The argument is given further support in another woman's account. She had been raped and beaten by a stranger. The day she returned from the hospital her husband, in front of their children, threw her on the bed and said "If that's what you wanted, why didn't you come to *me*?" In later days the woman, still injured, refused her husband's sexual approach. She relates that he responded "I have rights and you're my wife, and so long as you're my wife it is my conjugal right. So don't fight me." She didn't and then and later he angrily took what he wanted--he raped her. Russell comments: "Prior to the rape, he apparently held his sadistic urges in check, but when his wife was raped by someone else, he was no longer willing or able to do so."

In looking at the themes that run through these many and various accounts, Russell says that "conformity to traditional notions of femininity makes women more vulnerable to rape." She notes in particular that women are taught to be submissive to men, passive, and to think of themselves as weak and men as strong. Women are discouraged from learning to fight or even to show their anger to such a degree that Russell argues "unlearning to not fight is equally as important as learning to fight."

Women are also taught to be kind, compassionate, patient, and accepting. While these qualities are fine in themselves, Russell argues they can contribute to women's victimization. She cites numerous examples from the accounts in which compassion was repaid with violence. She also notes examples in which, having been trained to take responsibility for men, women accept, understand and tolerate the violence done to them by their husbands, lovers and male friends. She concludes: "Many women need to put more effort into protecting themselves rather than men's egos."

Russell does two things in this book. First, she provides a forum for women to tell their stories. In so doing, she affirms that women's voices are important, that we can and should listen and learn from women's descriptions of their experience.

Second, she explains some of the "whys" of that experience, by drawing out the commonalities of those descriptions and locating them within the cultural training of women as feminine. In accomplishing both these things Russell has made an enormous contribution to our understanding of both the experience and the meaning of sexual assault.

Warshaw, Robin. *I Never Called It Rape: The Ms. Report on Recognizing, Fighting and Surviving Date and Acquaintance Rape.* **New York: Harper and Row, 1988. 229 pages, indexed.**

This is a very readable book--the language is accessible, the format clear, and virtually all of the author's statements are supported by women's own descriptions. Statistical data are presented in such a way as to be optional for the reader--for the most part set out in boxed bold print, summing up and giving numerical validity to the text without interrupting the narrative flow. The clearly identified audiences are survivors of acquaintance rape, their friends and other supporters, and parents and counsellors.

Though based on a large-scale survey done for the *Ms.* Foundation by Mary P. Koss, this book is much more than a statistical report on incidence, demographics, etc. Building from that survey, Robin Warshaw interviewed or received written narratives from 150 women, survivors of date or acquaintance rape. Their stories suffuse the text, giving meaning and substance to the numbers and to Warshaw's analysis.

In defining acquaintance rape Warshaw is clear both that it is an act of violence and that it is a violence men do to women. She describes how, from the rapists' point of view, women they are dating or whom they already know are "safe" victims, that is, unlikely to offer serious resistance or to report the crime after the fact. More importantly, Warshaw discusses how women are taught to be "safe" victims and how men are taught to rape. Women are socialized to be passive, unassertive and dependent on men for physical and economic protection. They are also taught to view their sexuality as the barter with which to buy that protection. Men, on the other hand, are taught to be self-centered and single-minded in their pursuit of sex. Warshaw comments that men "view their relationships with women as adversarial challenges and learn to use both their physical and social power to overcome these smaller, less important people."

Warshaw discusses in some detail how women's conditioning leads to common reactions for women before, during and after an acquaintance rape. These reactions may include denial, dissociation, self-blame, ignoring the "little voice" warning of danger, not fighting back, not reporting the attack, and becoming a victim again. This discussion is typical of the book as a whole, for in it Warshaw blends a social analysis with women's own descriptions to create a convincing picture of both the what and the why of women's experience.

In later chapters of the book Warshaw takes a practical approach to acquaintance rape. Building on the description and analysis of earlier chapters she discusses ways for women to avoid or prevent acquaintance rape, what to do if you are raped, and ways to help survivors. She also discusses the responsibilities of parents, schools and lawmakers to deal with the issue and, in a separate and somewhat weaker chapter, discusses the changes men need to make in their attitudes and behaviour toward women. This practical approach, together with the grounded analysis and accessible language and presentation, make this book an excellent resource on what is too often a hidden or misunderstood issue of violence against women.

Other Useful Texts

Ellis, Megan. *Surviving Procedures After a Sexual Assault, Third Edition.* **Vancouver, Press Gang Publishers, 1988. 142 pages, not indexed.**

A handbook for survivors and rape crisis workers on medical, police and court procedures following a sexual assault. The third edition incorporates 1988 amendments to the Criminal Code regarding sexual offenses against children. Also includes a section on sexual harassment at work. The book explains the roles of the various actors--Crown Counsel, etc.--and the choices survivors have at each step in clear, readable language.

Gunn, Rita & Candice Minch. *Sexual Assault: The Dilemma of Disclosure, The Question of Conviction.* **Winnipeg: University of Manitoba Press, 1988. 148 pages, indexed.**

A new Canadian book that looks at victims' experience of

sexual assault, the social context, the role of the criminal justice
system, and an analysis of new sexual assault legislation.
Unfortunately, the writing is very academic, making the text
less usable than it might be.

Russell, Diana E.H. *Rape in Marriage.*
**New York: MacMillan, 1982. 412 pages,
indexed.**

An excellent description and analysis of an aspect of male
violence that too often slips through the cracks between wife
battering and sexual assault. Russell argues that "the continuum of violence and the continuum of sex merge in the act of wife
rape." Somewhat hard to get through--lots of statistics and
rather formal writing style--but well worth the effort.

Picture: Prostitution

Prostitution is a confusing issue. Along with pornography, it is at once the most public and most invisible issue of violence against women. We don't know enough from the women and children in prostitution about who they are and what their experience is. We need to hear more of their stories. As an issue of violence against women prostitution is also complicated by the fact that so many boys are involved. To the extent that those boys are treated as women their experience is similar to that of girls and women but precisely because they are boys their experience is also different. Yet too often their presence and their experience go unrecognized.

The issue is further complicated by the fact that many women involved in prostitution say it is their choice and they want their choice respected. As feminists we cannot dismiss their voices. We cannot tell them they are wrong. We must understand, however, that if daily exposure to violence and humiliation is a choice, then the alternatives must seem pretty horrible. And we must balance what the women in prostitution say with what those who have escaped it say.

Some women in prostitution have begun organizing. Of these, some see prostitution as a system of violence and seek to destroy it. Others view prostitution as a profession or a trade and lobby for improved working conditions or even unionization. There are different perspectives on prostitution, just as there are different perspectives on pornography. It is important to recognize these different perspectives, and not override or dismiss any woman's voice.

The picture of prostitution we present is incomplete. At this point we have more questions than answers. What is clear, though, is that when men buy women's and children's bodies, when they hurt those bodies, when they degrade and humiliate the people within those bodies, what they do is violence. That is the perspective of this picture.

To develop this picture, to learn as directly as possible about women's experience of prostitution as male violence, we went to three sources. We spoke to two women, a street worker and a private counsellor, who work with women and children in prostitution. Their knowledge and viewpoint, based on their experience, form the substance of the picture. We supplemented what they told us with information derived from a recording of a workshop given by Sarah Wynter, an American woman once involved in prostitution, now a feminist activist "engaged in revolt" against the system of prostitution. Third, we looked at "Bad Tricks Sheets" put out by prostitutes' rights groups which describe and warn of particularly dangerous tricks.

To begin, the workers told us that, from their perspective, prostitution is not a job like any other job. It is not a career choice--it is exploitation and abuse of women, girls, and boys who are treated as women. These people are beaten with hammers, lead pipes, fists, raped with penises and rifles, strangled, robbed, forced to do "disgusting and degrading" things. They describe a fourteen year old girl having her breasts slashed by a trick wielding a straight razor. They speak of fellatio, gang rapes, "hand jobs," "pussy fucks," children and women forced to eat shit or to act like a dog. They say each time a woman or girl or boy gets in a car she/he risks not coming back. The violence and abuse comes from virtually everyone these people encounter: from tricks, pimps, boyfriends, passersby, drug dealers, other prostitutes. Sometimes physical and sexual abuse also comes from the professionals--the lawyers, police, social workers and counsellors--who are supposed to be helping these women and children.

In the workers' experience, "nobody" gets into prostitution without the "initiation" of child sexual abuse. Young people escaping physical or mental abuse in the home may sell drugs, panhandle, do anything to survive rather than get involved in prostitution. The people who end up in prostitution have been sexualized and have "bought" the offender's description of the sexual abuse. The workers say the offenders' early training of them means the victims' identity is wrapped up in what the abusers told them was their "sexual dangerousness" and their attractiveness.

According to the workers, for a child who has been sexually

abused prostitution represents reality. It reflects and therefore normalizes her experience of abuse. This function of normalizing and making the past real is tremendously important to the child or woman. Prostitution also means a kind of freedom. A child who is sexually abused by her father has no power or control over what is done to her, even if she is told it is her fault. That same child sexually abused by a stranger for money feels herself to have power: she chooses when and for how long, she puts a dollar value to it, but most importantly, she has the freedom to hate the man, something she is not allowed to feel about her father-abuser. That sense of power and control is tremendously important to one who has always been powerless. The workers say it lasts until, for example, a trick pulls a razor, thereby demonstrating through violence who really has the power in prostitution.

The workers say that like other victims of child sexual abuse, women and children in prostitution feel damaged, ashamed, bad, without value. The longer they stay in prostitution the more that becomes their identity--they see themselves as prostitutes only, unable to do or be anything else. They become defeated people whose only positive experience in life is being recognized as attractive by a trick. These people endure the damage done to their bodies and souls by not experiencing it. They use drugs, forget, become void; they separate or dissociate. They maintain a front of being tough and together, telling themselves that what they are doing is okay, that they are fine. That front is essential to their survival; they cannot afford to feel anything, including physical pain. Some of the people in prostitution compartmentalize the pain in their lives either by developing multiple personalities or by changing their names each time they are hurt. When these tactics don't work--and they can't work consistently--the workers say the women and children use violence to block pain. Girls and women slash themselves, boys break their hands in fights or against walls. Some finally kill themselves.

The men who buy women's and children's bodies are every age and class and occupation and category of men imaginable. They are teachers and lawyers and judges and doctors. They are "the weird old asshole when he gets his cheque," the "punk in his Camero out to impress his friends." They are loggers and ship workers--men who spend most of their time working in isolated settings and so have no expectations of having an ongoing relationship with a woman. The workers say that most commonly, the men are between twenty-five and forty years old, married with children whom they likely also abuse. From the

62

workers' perspective, in buying what is to them a faceless body, these men are seeking a greater power difference, and hence stimulation for their egos than they get in their marriages. Some look for children to "feed off," rationalizing that these children are "damaged goods" and hence "safe" to abuse: "she's not a child, she's a hooker." Whether it's adult women or children, though, the workers say that what prompts all these men is the desire to humiliate. They cite the chilling awareness of one girl who said, "I realize that what they want is my shame."

The workers say that what the women and children in prostitution think of the men who use them is that they are "suckers" and "jerks" who give them money for something the women and children do not value--their sexuality. The women and children sneer at what they see as the men's desperation about their erect penises. They have no respect for the men, feel animosity and antagonism toward them, and are sometimes sickened by them, such as when a man must move his own child's safety seat in order to sexually use another child in the back of his car. And yet, the workers say, the women and children in prostitution need the men's money, need the affirmation of being found attractive. And some take the men's abuse in order to give meaning to the original abuse they suffered at home, to convince themselves that what their fathers and grandfathers did to them was normal.

Some readers may take exception to our inclusion of prostitution in this Guide. Some people, including some feminists, claim that prostitution is not an issue of violence against women. They say prostitution is a viable economic option for women, that selling your body on the street is no different than selling your labour in a factory, that prostitution is a job like any other. But having a rifle barrel shoved up your vagina is not an occupational hazard recognized by the Workers Compensation Board. Neither is AIDS or any other sexually transmitted disease. The picture of prostitution the workers give us is one of unrelenting, horrifying violence and degradation. We say prostitution is an issue of male violence because what happens to women and children in prostitution *is* violence.

It is a kind of violence many of us don't know about but which all of us are hurt by. It is a system of violence which allows and encourages men to see women and children as objects for consumption, to be bought, used and thrown away. If $50.00 buys a man the right to sexually hurt and humiliate a stranger, what is to prevent him from saving his money by doing the same things to those he already "owns"--his wife and children--or to any other available woman or child?

We began this picture by saying there are different perspectives on prostitution. Prostitutes' rights groups, which as a rule view prostitution as a profession or trade and which lobby for improved working conditions or unionization, do sometimes serve a purpose in validating who these women are, that they are more than "faceless fucks." But improving working conditions does not alter the fact that the so-called sex trade is trade in humiliation. As one American ex-prostitute put it: "Slavery is slavery. Unionizing the slaves is not the answer."

The Texts

Barry, Kathleen. *Female Sexual Slavery.* New York: Avon Books, 1979. 325 pages, indexed.

After ten years this book remains the classic feminist reference on both the international traffic in women and street prostitution. It documents the world-wide pervasiveness of sexual enslavement of women and children, describes the systematic violence and exploitation that is their lives, and traces the connections between female sexual slavery and other forms of violence against women. As a result, this book makes an enormous contribution to our understanding of patterns of male violence.

Barry defines female sexual slavery broadly, including all situations in which women and girls are entrapped, powerless and subject to sexual violence and exploitation. Using this definition, she discusses not only the organized trafficking in women's bodies and unorganized pimp-controlled street prostitution, but also wife assault and child sexual abuse within the family. She says that the social and political context within which women and girls are sexually enslaved is formed by what she calls the "rape paradigm"--a political crime of violence against women for which the victim herself is blamed. She goes on to say:

> Recognition of the commonality of women's experience in female sexual slavery breaks the time-honoured separation of women into competitive and incompatible categories of madonna and whore and makes its possible to understand that "victim" can mean also prostitute, battered wife, incestuously assaulted child, veiled woman, purchased bride.

This is a tremendously important insight, one which as feminists we may be aware of on some level but sometimes lose sight of as we focus our energies and attention on specific issues of violence against women. It is also important to remember, though, that there are differences, both within and among issues. To be kidnapped from Paris and sold at an auction in Zanzibar is a different experience than "turning out" on the street in San Francisco. Both of these experiences are different from that of a child sexually used by only one man--her father-- in the "comfort" of a suburban home. It does seem sometimes that in stressing the commonality of women's experience Barry passes over the differences. Given the scope of the book and the vividness of the patterns Barry discovered, it is an understandable oversight.

Another important contribution Barry makes to feminists' understanding of patterns of violence comes in her articulation of the concept of sexual terrorism. She says that because sexual violence by definition is unlimited, terror permeates the lives of all women, because all women are either victims or potential victims. She argues that for women terror is a way of life and a legacy passed from mother to daughter. Here Barry does make distinctions about different women's experiences. Potential victims alter their lives--install dead-bolt locks, wait for their children at bus stops--out of fear of what might happen to them. Victims experience first disbelief then terror during an assault. Then and later they struggle with such questions as, "Could this be happening to me, can I escape, why is this happening?" But, says Barry, if a woman is held in slavery, "terrorism becomes her 'normal' life and these questions have to be answered in some way that will enable her to cope with the immediate situation." Just as the situations of sexual terrorism vary so do women's survival tactics and Barry argues that to understand the latter we must first imagine the former. Only by appreciating the specific context of sexual terrorism can we come to recognize women's actions as active attempts at survival and hence avoid the mistake of "victimism" or victim-blaming.

Barry devotes a chapter to describing the methods by which men acquire and keep women in prostitution. She says procuring and pimping are "the crystallization of misogyny" and the methods used are the same in foreign traffic and local prostitution. The five patterns she identifies are: befriending or love; actions of groups, syndicates or organized crime; employment agencies; purchase; and kidnapping. In this Barry's description differs from the picture the workers we talked to gave us. They said that most girls and women in prostitution do not have pimps--though they may have boyfriends they support--and that generally they are not actively recruited or forced into prostitution. (Force, they said, is much more a factor with boys.) The informants did note that the situation has been changing in the last two years, that there are now more pimps and more women working for pimps, and they speculated that this may be because of the increased drug trade.

Barry does reflect our informants' description when she discusses the influence of prior abuse on women in prostitution. She says that when a child is physically, sexually, and/or psychologically abused, she comes to see herself and her body as her abusers do, as someone and something worthy of such treatment. As an adult, she does not like, need or want the abuse she suffers in prostitution but, in Barry's words, she has developed the "self-image of a throwaway." Throwaway women are women who, once given the definition of prostitute, are "recycled into the world, where they are used and abused and disposed of when no longer of use." That image of women's bodies being like no deposit/no return bottles is similar to activist Sarah Wynter's analogy of an old diaphragm: "fuck it until it's no good then throw it away and get another one."

Throughout the text, most particularly in her discussion of pornography and the "ideology of cultural sadism" and "sex colonization," Barry emphatically attributes violence against women to the male "sex-is-power ethic." In this context she says that female sexual slavery is a way of men controlling women, either directly through enslavement or indirectly through the threat of enslavement. Whether the form of slavery is forced prostitution, arranged marriage or wife battering, the effect is the same: the potential or present reality of each form for all women serves to keep power in the hands of men individually and as a sex-class.

This is a wide-ranging book, both geographically and analytically. It is, as Gloria Steinem says, a "crusading book," for it reveals what has been hidden and explains what it exposes such that the perpetrators--men--are called to account. Barry says: "Knowing the worst frees us to hope and strive for the best." With this book Barry inspires and enables all of us concerned about violence against women to do just that.

Barry, Kathleen. "Social Etiology of Crimes Against Women," in *Victimology: An International Journal*, Vol. 10, 1985, pp.164-173.

Written for an academic journal, this article provides a very good analysis of misogyny and sex-power, particularly as they relate to prostitution. The crimes of sexual violence against women Barry includes in her definition are: rape, wife battering, child sexual abuse, sexual harassment, pornography, and prostitution. She says in each of these the aggressor "unites sex and violence to subdue, humiliate, degrade and terrorize his female victim." She argues that these crimes against women originate in the way male sexuality is socially constructed. In particular, she says that because men as a class hold power over women as a class, male sexuality is socially defined to link violence and sex.

Barry says that prostitution has not been considered a crime against women because the prostitute is seen "either as a willing participant or as a criminal herself." In response, Barry outlines the coercive methods used to recruit and keep women in prostitution. She then looks at the experience of women in prostitution, whether their involvement is forced or apparently freely chosen. She says that those women don't experience what is done to them in prostitution as sex. Like rape victims and children who are sexually abused, Barry says women in prostitution separate themselves and their feelings from their bodies, mentally retreating to a place that cannot be touched. She characterizes this process as "the human refusal of total objectification." It is, then, a survival tactic, but one which has as a consequence a "schizophrenic split in the self."

Men do not buy women, they buy women's body parts--objects to be acted upon. But, says Barry, this commoditized sex, whether it is bought in prostitution or seized in rape, "is sex to the aggressor." In other words, Barry argues that men experience sexual violence as sex, while at the same time blaming the victim for what they do to her.

Barry says that through the work of feminists there is now more social awareness of the crimes of wife battering and rape. On these issues it is now less easy to blame the victim. Prostitution laws, on the other hand, continue to punish the victim while ignoring the crimes of the pimps and consumers. Additionally, Barry argues that men's right to exercise their socially learned, distorted sexuality has been condemned in the case of rape but continues to be accepted in the case of prostitution. As a result, prostitution remains the "institutionalized validation of rape and sexual violence."

This article is very dense--a lot of ideas packed into a small space and presented in rather academic language. It is, though, a challenging and thought-provoking perspective on prostitution as a sexual crime against women.

Wynter, Sarah. "Whisper: Women Hurt in Systems of Prostitution Engaged in Revolt," in Frederique Delacoste & Priscilla Alexander, eds., *Sex Work: Writings by Women in the Sex Industry.* Pittsburgh: Cleis Press, 1987, pp.266-270.

Sarah Wynter brings to her work both personal experience and knowledge of many other women's stories. Having herself escaped from prostitution, she founded WHISPER to assist other women to escape, to document the truth about women's experience of prostitution as a system of male violence, and, ultimately, to destroy that system.

Wynter says that prostitution is not a "victimless" crime or a crime of women. It is a crime committed by men against women. She says prostitution is founded on "enforced sexual abuse under a system of male supremacy." That system lies about women in prostitution, just as it lies about rape victims, battered wives and sexually abused children. The lies, says Wynter, are the same in all cases: "They want it. They like it. If they didn't they would leave."

Wynter comments on prostitution's links with other issues of violence against women on both experiential and ideological levels. She notes, for example, that upwards of seventy-five per cent of women in prostitution were sexually abused as children and that sexual assault and battering are common experiences. She also points to the ways societal institutions--the church, the state--and political factions--the conservative right, the liberal left--all "collude" to teach women prostitution by supporting men's right to sexually own and violate women and children. In particular, Wynter discusses prostitution's link with pornography. The two are interdependent. Pornography sanctions the commercial sexual exploitation of women and children, thereby teaching prostitution. At the same time, pornography cannot exist without prostitution. Wynter concludes: "It is impossible to separate pornography from prostitution. The acts are identical except that in pornography there is a permanent record of the woman's abuse."

This article reads rather like a manifesto. As such, it is less a detailed description of women's experience of prostitution than an unadorned, uncompromising truth-telling exercise about the meaning of prostitution and its place in the pattern of male violence against women.

68

Other Useful Texts

**Bracey, Dorothy H. "Concurrent and Con-
secutive Abuse: The Juvenile Prostitute,"
in Barbara Raffel Price & Natalie J. Sokoloff,
eds., *The Criminal Justice System and
Women*. New York: Clark Boardman, 1982,
pp.317-322.**

This article notes the incidence of child sexual abuse, aban-
donment and rape in the histories of girls and young women in
prostitution. It also describes violence from boyfriends and from
tricks and punitive treatment by institutions. Bracey concludes, "As long as we pretend that incest and the seduction of
children are rare events, as long as juvenile prostitution is
viewed as an act of delinquency rather than as a manifestation
of social and cultural forces that lead to troubled teenage young
girls, it will not be possible to examine and deal with child
prostitution realistically."

**Fraser, Lynn. *Toward an Understanding
of Prostitution*. Calgary: Calgary Alliance
for the Safety of Prostitutes, undated. 22
pages, not indexed.**

This booklet provides a good and clear description of the three
legislative options available regarding prostitution: decrimi-
nalization, legalization, and criminalization. Also includes a
sample Bad Trick Sheet. The author sees prostitution as both
an economic issue and an issue of violence against women, and
reflects both in her proposals for change.

Picture: Pornography

Writing a picture of women's experience of pornography is made difficult by the paradoxical fact that in spite of pornography's ubiquity, the women in pornography are invisible. If, as Kathleen Barry says, the women in prostitution are throwaway women, the women in pornography are the already discarded: all we see of them are photographic, film and video records of their abuse. Furthermore, in addition to the women in pornography, the picture must also include the experience of women upon whom pornography is used. And, because pornography so powerfully influences social definitions of sexuality, we need to know about the women pornography affects, which is all of us.

To write this picture we went to three sources. We read the account of a woman who was used in and eventually escaped from the pornography industry--Linda Marchiano. We looked at interviews with child sexual abuse survivors and with women who have been sexually harassed at work for their experiences of pornography. And we spoke to an anti-pornography activist.

For many sexually abused children pornography forms part of their environment, even if it is not used directly in the abuse. Some adult survivors recall that the abusers casually displayed pictures of "asses and breasts" and magazines such as Playboy and Penthouse. Some say they were encouraged to read what was left lying about. Other women say the abusers showed them films and pictures and in some cases directed the child to do what was in the picture. We contend that even in the absence of direct instruction the effect of such exposure is to inappropriately sexualize a child and to teach her what men believe women and children are for. In other cases it seems pornography is used simply for the abuser's "edification" or "benefit." For example, an adult survivor recalls that her uncle always read pornography while he was sexually abusing her. Others say the abuser took photographs of them or their body parts, thereby creating his own pornography.

Some survivors of child sexual abuse say that for a time as adults they used pornography themselves because, in linking humiliation and arousal, it replicated their childhood experience. Through their early training they had learned that to be sexual is to be powerless, to be trapped, to be abused. As adults they found that they could feel sexual only if they also felt those things and pornography helped them do that. At the same time, though, they found using pornography made them feel disgusted, ashamed and angry and, therefore, unable or unwilling to be sexual.

Women say that pornography plays a significant role in their experience of workplace sexual harassment. Their male coworkers and supervisors display pornographic photographs-- women masturbating, for example--in common work areas and sometimes write comments across the bodies of the women depicted. Women say when they are confronted with these pictures they feel offended, humiliated or as if they are being "subjected to [someone else's] sexual fantasies." Most often, if they object to such displays, the women are laughed at or called prudes by the men. If they try to have the pornography removed they are treated with hostility.

The experiences of all these women are reflected in the comments of an anti-pornography activist. She describes children being forced to watch and perform pornography. She recalls a study in which convicted sex offenders described their use of pornography as an "instigator," something to get them aroused before they raped. In recounting women's experiences of being exposed to pornography she says they are frightened to learn that men look on women as "sexual automatons." In her opinion, given the incidence of rape, wife battering and child sexual abuse, women are right to be frightened, because pornography reinforces "male superiority" and the philosophy that "sex is dirty, sex is women, therefore women are dirty."

This activist identifies the heaviest users of pornography as teenaged and young adult men. For them pornography is sex instruction, a truly frightening thought. Of the other users she says they are ordinary men who bully. In her work she has seen the results--bullied women are women silent and afraid. Pornography is part of the bullying.

One of the arguments used by the pro-pornography lobby is that the women used in pornography are there by choice. They point to smiling faces in the films and pictures to "prove" that those women enjoy what is done to them. It is, of course, a spurious argument to claim that if the victim "likes" it, it isn't violence. More to the point, though, the argument is a lie, one which Linda Marchiano has sought to expose.

Marchiano details the horrifying and unrelenting physical, sexual and verbal abuse used to create pornography's smiling images. She describes being "raped, beaten, punched, smacked, choked, degraded, and yelled at" daily by her pimp/pornographer husband. She lists his threats if she didn't do what he told her to: that he would cut her face, that he would shoot her or strangle her, that he would kill her parents. This man, Chuck Traynor, taught Marchiano to relax her muscles so she could take a man's penis in her throat; this act became the film "Deep Throat." In other films she was forced to perform sexually with women and, a degradation which still haunts her, with a dog.

She describes enduring physical pain and humiliation by using drugs and numbing herself, becoming a "zombie." Marchiano performed in pornography by choice, but the choice was one of life or death. Her husband said: "You make this movie or you're going to die," and to ensure she understood her options, kept a gun within her view, though out of the camera's. Her smiles in the films are there because she learned "a false smile was a lot better than a real beating," not to mention death.

The Texts

Cole, Susan G. *Pornography and the Sex Crisis.* Toronto: Amanita, 1989. 182 pages, not indexed.

A new Canadian book which presents a radical feminist analysis of pornography--what it is, what it does, who it hurts, and what can be done about it. Though the subject is theoretical, Cole's language is clear, reasonably accessible and often powerful.

In a sense, it seems Cole's project in this book is to set the record straight. In Canada especially, feminists who fight pornography are too often depicted as pro-censorship and anti-sex--repressed, naive and too willing to give over control to the state. In dismantling that misconception, Cole begins by describing what pornography is. It's an obvious starting point but one which too often has been lost in the great censorship debates of recent years. For the purposes of this Guide, it is the most important section of the book.

Like American feminists Andrea Dworkin and Catharine MacKinnon, Cole says that pornography is not words and pictures; it is "a practice of sexual subordination in which women's inferior status is eroticized and thus maintained." As a practice, pornography teaches men to derive sexual pleasure from women's subordination. Part of that teaching is experiential, for pornography is not just seen, it is felt. It creates not just images or fantasies but erect penises for the men who purchase it.

In defining pornography as a practice of sexual subordination, Cole addresses simultaneously three misconceptions. First, pornography is not just sex or sexual explicitness, and, therefore, is not just a matter of good or poor taste, community standards, etc. Neither is pornography just violence. A graphic war movie may be horrible and horrifying; it may be offensive. It is not pornographic. Finally, not all pornography is explicitly violent, though certainly as an instrument of subordination violence is much favoured by men, both in pornography and in other male practices. So pornography is not sex, not violence, and not always the linking of sex and violence. It is "the active subordination of the most degraded female slaves."

Cole explicitly states that one of the fundamental principles underlying her analysis is that women matter. That principle suffuses the text and Cole returns to it repeatedly. The women used in the production of pornography matter. They are its immediate victims but too often, says Cole, they are seen as "pornography's collaborators." Pornography documents some, but certainly not all, of the abuse those women suffer. Usually, they are women trapped in systems of prostitution--women for whom there are not other options, women trained for sexual abuse from childhood.

The women upon whom pornography is used also matter. Cole describes, for example, the experiences of battered women forced to buy, look at, and replicate the activities in their husband's pornographic materials. She also describes how child rapists use pornography to train children in sexual compliance. The women used in pornography's production and the women upon whom pornography is used are connected by abuse: "women are abused to make the materials that (male) customers use in ways that are abusive to women." When children are added to the equation, the cycle is complete: "What happens is that pornography increases the appeal of child sexual abuse, which is then acted out on children, which in turn helps create the population of women who will wind up in the pornography of the future."

Pornography lies about women, about men, and about sex. For women the greatest lie in pornography is that women want to be sexually abused--raped, tortured, beaten, humiliated. Pornography teaches men that what men want to do to women is what women want done to them: "In the world of pornography, men take women, hurt women, fuck them and use them, while women are hurt, fucked, used and enjoy it." Thus, pornography constructs a sexuality of dominance and submission, a sexuality that is not just fantasized but practised. Cole concludes: "Pornography is an effective agent of social control, and the lies of pornography are becoming the truth about life."

Cole describes how pornography portrays different "categories" of women, especially women of colour and lesbians. She says that pornography "eroticizes racism," by showing black women in scenarios of slavery and Asian women in pornography of "torture and ultra-passivity." Lesbian sexuality is depicted not as a freely chosen option but rather as a desperate act of sex-starved women who don't have access to men. Cole says that in video pornography the women are often interrupted by one or two men who give them "what they really need." In either scenario pornography gives the male consumer "not one but two women to whom he can have sexual access, two women he can metaphorically fuck, use and enjoy."

When Cole looks at pornography produced by and for lesbians and gay men she finds the same ideology of dominance and submission and the same gendered sexuality: "The sexes are the same but the roles remain different--masculine and feminine, powerful and powerless."

In the second section of the book Cole translates her analysis of pornography into concrete proposals for change. In particular, she outlines seven feminist criteria to be met by anti-pornography laws:

1.) Consider pornography a practice, not merely pictures, words or ideas.
2.) Target the harm women experience.
3.) Make the law women-centred and not gender-neutral.
4.) Make the law women-initiated and women-driven.
5.) Compensate the victims of pornography.
6.) Advance gender equality.

7.)   Permit artistic and educational dialogue on sexuality.

This civil remedies approach is similar to that taken by Dworkin and MacKinnon in the Minneapolis Ordinanace. Given Canada's rather different political culture--tending to be more authoritarian and inclined to look to the state to protect and mediate among citizens--this approach may not be as effective here as in the United States. It has the great advantage, though, of keeping control in the hands of women rather than the state, and so of making the issue of censorship largely irrelevant.

The depth of Cole's thinking, and the care with which she presents it, make this a tremendously important book. Cole is respectful of the women whose experience she describes and in most cases respectful of the women with whom she disagrees. Distinctly radical, it is a book to be pondered, struggled with and appreciated by all of us concerned about pornography as an issue of violence against women.

Dworkin, Andrea. *Pornography: Men Possessing Women*. New York: Perigee Books, 1981. 300 pages, indexed.

This is a difficult book to read. The language, while certainly accessible, at times borders on a barrage. It is unrelenting, unadorned, and in its bluntness puts us in the place of the women Dworkin talks about. For an uncompromising feminist analysis of pornography, though, this book is one of the best.

One of the difficulties many feminists have with the issue of pornography is that we literally don't know what we're talking about. That is, we don't know the content of pornography because we don't read the books or watch the films and videos. Part of what makes Dworkin's work so authoritative and powerful is that throughout the text she describes pornography's content, using pornography's language. It is a horrifying litany of sexual abuse and degradation, one which we must confront.

Dworkin not only describes what pornography is, she explains what it means and what it does. She locates pornography within the social and historical context of male supremacy and, more specifically, within the male ideology of sexual violence. She says, for example, that for men, "the right to abuse women is elemental, the first principle." Pornography reinforces that belief in part by blaming the victim, by telling men that "sexual violence is desired by the normal female, needed by her, suggested or demanded by her." In practice, this means women cannot be victims for if the true nature of woman is "harlot," desiring to be sexually controlled, then "nothing that signifies that nature is either violating or victimizing." Accordingly, for men rape is not rape; it is what women want and need.

Dworkin says that one of the ways pornography teaches men to see women as sexually insatiable and desiring of abuse is through its depiction of supposed lesbian sexuality. With no man in the picture, it appears the viewer is seeing women "as they really are." How women are, according to pornography, is sadistic, masochistic, evil and craven.

Dworkin says that the raison d'etre of pornography is male power. That power has many aspects, listed by Dworkin as: "the power of self, physical power over and against others, the power of terror, the power of naming, the power of owning, the power of money, and the power of sex." One way or another all of these aspects of male power are expressed in pornography. What pornography teaches is that the way for individual men to achieve male power is to sexually use, abuse, degrade, humiliate and subordinate women.

Dworkin argues that the social encouragement of men's sexual violence against women serves a purpose: protecting men and boys from male sexual abuse. She supports this argument in part by pointing to the differential treatment afforded the sexual abuse of boys and men versus girls and women. No doubt Dworkin is right that assaults on the former are seen as more serious than assaults on the latter because boys and men are socially valued in a way girls and women are not. The point Dworkin fails to make, though, is that when boys and men are sexually assaulted by men they are treated as women-- weak and therefore abusable, gendered female. It is no accident that men raped in prison and boys and men raped in gay male pornography are referred to as "she," as Cole and others have pointed out. Treating a man or boy as female, then, is another way for men to achieve male power.

The subject of racism appears repeatedly in Dworkin's text. She discusses the meaning and importance of using black women in pornography in the "race-bound" society of the United States. She highlights ethnic stereotypes of, for example, gypsies and Poles in the pornography she describes. She also discusses at some length the racism that is anti-semitism. She says that the "sexualization of 'the Jewess' in cultures that abhor Jews--subtly or overtly--is the paradigm for the sexualization of all racially or ethnically degraded women." More than that, Dworkin asserts that the image of the Jewish concentration camp woman, the record and memory of her sexual degradation "is at the heart of the sadism against all women that is now promoted in mainstream sexual propaganda."

Though she does not specifically propose how to overthrow what she calls the "imperial power" of men in pornography, Dworkin contends that overcoming silence is crucial. In the concluding paragraph of the book she says:

> The boys are betting on our compliance, our ignorance, our fear. We have always refused to face the worst that men have done to us. The boys count on it. The boys are betting that we cannot face the horror of their sexual system and survive. The boys are betting that their depictions of us as whores will beat us down and stop our hearts. The boys are betting that their penises and fists and knives and fucks and rapes will turn us into what they say we are--the compliant women of sex, the voracious cunts of pornography, the masochistic sluts who resist because we really want more. The boys are betting. The boys are wrong.

In writing this book, particularly in writing it using the language men use to describe women, Dworkin has created a space for all of us first to listen, and then to speak and to act for ourselves.

Other Useful Texts

Dworkin, Andrea & Catherine A. MacKinnon. *Pornography and Civil Rights: A New Day for Women's Equality.* **Minneapolis: Organizing Against Pornography, 1988. 142 pages, not indexed.**

A practical guide, written in accessible language, on the civil remedies approach to fighting pornography. It includes a good section dealing with common questions about pornography. Written for an American audience, the book is not immediately applicable to Canadian feminists but provides useful background, especially for those interested in pursuing Cole's proposals for legislative change.

77

MacKinnon, Catharine A. *Feminism Unmodified: Discourses on Life and Law.* **Cambridge: Harvard University Press, 1987. 315 pages, indexed.**

A third of the speeches in this collection concern pornography. MacKinnon says pornography is not just imagery but "sexual reality," and that it harms "many women one at a time and helps keep all women in an inferior status by defining our subordination as our sexuality and equating that with our gender." See annotation in Patterns of Violence section.

Marchiano (Lovelace), Linda, with Mike McGrady. *Ordeal.* **New York: Berkley Books, 1981. 263 pages, not indexed.**

A horrifying first person account of a woman imprisoned in systems of prostitution and pornography and her eventual escape. A stunning rebuttal to those who claim women in pornography are there by choice. Written for a popular audience, it is accessible without being sensational. A painful and necessary book to read.

YWCA of Metropolitan Toronto. *Who Says It Doesn't Hurt?: A Manual for Workshop Leaders.* **Toronto: YWCA, 1988. 59 pages, not indexed.**

Intended to accompany a video of the same name, this book describes how to facilitate a workshop on pornography, questions and answers about pornography, and provides the text of the video. Also lists Toronto-area resources and a short bibliography.

Picture: Patterns of Violence

When we look at all the pictures of women's experience of different forms of male violence patterns emerge. This picture is about those patterns. It is different from the other pictures in being more wide-ranging, less specifically descriptive and more analytical, more engaged in the complexities--the commonalities, variations and differences--of the issues. This picture describes what we have learned in preparing this Guide.

The most obvious thread that runs through all the pictures is that the violence women experience is sex violence and sexual violence. It is sex violence, analogous to sex discrimination, inasmuch as girls and women are targetted for violence precisely because they are female and therefore vulnerable and subordinate. Furthermore, it is sexual violence in that it is directed at women and girls in their sexual beings, most often specifically at the parts of their bodies considered to be sexual--breasts and genitals and mouths.

The second obvious thread is that women and girls suffer violence at the hands of men. Overwhelmingly in women's accounts it is men who rape, men who batter their girlfriends and wives, men who sexually abuse children, men who sexually harass their female co-workers and employees, men who buy sexual access to women's and children's bodies in prostitution and pornography. There are exceptions. Some women are abusive to their husbands, though those men usually have greater options for leaving the situation than do battered women. A few women sexually abuse female and male children, though their motivations apparently are different from men's. Some women, a very few, buy boys' bodies in the prostitution called escort services. And we are learning that some lesbians beat and sexually assault their partners. We do not discount in any way the harm these women cause to other women and children, and sometimes to men. Indeed, more work is needed to understand these realities from the perspective of women. The fact remains, however, that in women's accounts and in the literature, the vast majority of abusers of women and children are men.

When women describe their responses to the sexual violence men do to them they say very similar things, often using the same words. They talk about fear, especially fear generated by unpredictability, by never knowing whether or when the next attack will come. Women talk about blaming themselves for the violence men do to them. They blame themselves for "provoking" their attackers, blame themselves for getting into the situation, blame themselves for having something evil or bad inside them that would cause a man to hurt them.

Related to self-blame is shame. Women talk a lot about shame. Too often, in their shame they are silent, powerless to name, to speak, to act to end the abuse they suffer. Shame means women feel unworthy of protection and healing. So they are silent and in their silence wait for the next attack, if not from this man then from another. Some women say they feel marked, that having once been victimized, they are destined always to be men's victims. For some women, especially those sexually abused as children, each new assault serves to reaffirm their belief that they caused the original abuse, that it was their fault and abuse is all they are good for, all they deserve. For many women that reaffirmation can be a daily event.

Whether a woman is sexually attacked once by a stranger or repeatedly by her husband, father, co-worker or many strangers, the experience changes how she looks at men. Even those women who explain the violence to themselves as an isolated incident or the act of one bad or sick man describe feeling wary of men in general. They say they feel less trusting; they might fear intimacy, or have a greater need to protect themselves physically and psychologically. Many women say that their experience of sexual violence led them to believe that all men are abusive. For a child whose knowledge of love and of sex comes from her sexually abusive father it is a logical conclusion. So too for the child or woman assaulted repeatedly by the men who buy her body. The conclusion, though, is shared by many other women, by women raped and beaten by their boyfriends and husbands, by women for whom every new job is a new "battlefield" of sexual harassment. Listening to all these women's stories, it's hard to say their conclusion is wrong.

A theme not spoken of directly in all the pictures is the economic consequences of men's sexual violence. Some women who are sexually harassed say that they were threatened with losing promotions or even their jobs if they did not submit to their supervisors' sexual demands. Others quit their jobs to escape sexual harassment. For women and children in prostitution, some of whom are also used in producing pornography, the lack of economic options contributes to their entrapment. For battered women, having no control over money can be part of the abuse they suffer, and escaping their batterers can mean poverty for them and their children. And for all the victims of male violence, for child sexual abuse survivors and rape victims and all the rest, recovery often requires the assistance of a counsellor or support services. When services are not provided by the community, or when services are provided but are inadequate, women must pay for private counselling, sometimes for years. Women who can't pay go without.

Another theme that stands out in the pictures has to do with the ways women endure and survive the often horrendous violence men inflict on them. By now they are familiar, for example: a sexually abused child dissociates, separates her self from her body; a battered woman drinks or uses prescription or other drugs to numb the fear and the pain; a woman in prostitution changes her name each time she is hurt; a sexually harassed woman pretends nothing happened, willing herself to forget, and on and on. Often these methods are considered "maladaptive" by professionals and others. They are used to label women "crazy" or used as "proof" that the woman is masochistic, that she wants the abuse she suffers and therefore is to blame for it. We say these methods are survival skills and that they are signs of health. They tell of feistiness, inventiveness, strength, and a fundamental valuing of self. The same can be said of the many ways women try to avoid or halt men's violence: an abused child runs whenever she can, a sexually harassed woman quits her job, a battered woman suggests marriage counselling. Even suicide says "I will not live this constant abuse."

This leads to the next theme of the pictures we want to talk about. It has to do with the importance of meaning. All women, whether they are raped or battered or trapped in prostitution or whatever, try to make sense of the violence they suffer. They try to explain it to themselves. They say, "I wasn't nice enough, I talked back and so he hit me." They say, "He was sick, he suffered abuse as a child." They say, "All men are like that, it's a woman's lot." Experiencing male sexual violence once or a hundred times is confusing. Sometimes women can't even trust that it really happened, especially when abusers and some professionals tell them they imagined it all. Sometimes for their own survival women try to convince themselves that it didn't happen or that if it did it "wasn't so bad." But making sense of the violence is vital for women to truly survive and live free of its effects. Women must know and believe that the violence was real, that it wasn't their fault or for their benefit, and that they are not alone in struggling to survive. We all need to know that male violence is real, that it is men's responsibility, and that it affects us all.

Something not described in the pictures is what the academics call "multiple victimization." We have found that many women experience more than one kind of male violence at the hands of different men at different points in their lives. Women also witness other women being hurt by men. It's something difficult to describe without being left open to charges of sensationalism or adding grist to the mill of "victim precipitation" theories, which say that somehow women and children "attract" or "provoke" the violence done to them. There is also a niggling doubt that we may not be believed. But the stories, taken from interviews with battered wives, young women assaulted in dating relationships and child sexual abuse survivors, are true and they must be told:

A child is beaten by her father. Her mother's boyfriend threatens/attempts to throw her out an eighteenth storey window. At age thirteen the child is raped by a friend of her sister's boyfriend. At age fifteen she is living on the street. Her boyfriend beats, verbally abuses and rapes her. He forces her into prostitution. She is beaten and raped by tricks. When she tells her boyfriend he ties her to a chair and rapes her. She is sixteen.

A child witnesses her step-father beating her mother regularly. The child and her siblings are threatened by their step-father. The child is sexually abused by her step-father. She grows up and the man she marries beats her. After she gives birth he beats their child.

A child is sexually abused by her uncle. In a foster home she is beaten by her foster father. She witnesses her foster father rape her sister. She herself is sexually abused by her foster brothers. The man she marries beats her, psychologically abuses her and threatens her. The next man she is involved with also threatens her.

A child watches her father beat her mother regularly, finally slitting her mother's throat. The child and her siblings are terrorized by their father. The child grows up and marries but the marriage doesn't last. She marries again but her second husband sexually abuses their daughter. She marries again but her third husband beats her, threatens her and rapes her.

A child is beaten and sexually abused by her father. As an adult she is raped by one man, sexually harassed by other men, and beaten by her husband.

A child and her siblings are beaten by their father. The child is sexually abused, beaten and sexually tortured by her uncle. The child is sexually abused by friends of her uncle. The child is prostituted by her uncle.

These stories are representative of many others. Many women, when asked to describe their experience of a particular form of male violence, mention, almost as an aside, other forms of violence they've experienced or witnessed. For some it seems that male violence is normalized, that in various forms it has been a part of their lives for so long that it is simply a part of the environment, part of being a woman. So, are these women right when they say, as some do, that prior victimization leaves them marked as a victim, that men have a radar and can pick them out for further abuse? Or is it simply that given the incidence of rape, battering, child sexual abuse, etc. that any woman's chance of being "hit on" more than once is high?

The answer is probably a combination of these. Men's targetting of some women is seen most clearly in the pictures of child sexual abuse and prostitution. A father, discovering that his daughter has been sexually abused by another man, rapes her as punishment. A man takes advantage of an already abused child's vulnerability and naivety, telling her that his sexual abuse will be healthy and beneficial to her. A grandfather "rescues" a child from her father's sexual abuse, and "protects" her from him by abusing her himself. Men rationalize buying women and children in prostitution by saying they are "damaged goods" and therefore "safe" to abuse. The women and children those men buy are in prostitution largely because of their early training in sexual abuse. And too often, when they seek the help of professionals, they are further sexually abused. Targetting is also seen in the pictures of dating violence, rape and sexual harassment, for example, when a woman objects to one man's abuse, he makes it public and other men join in the "fun."

Beyond targetting, though, is the simple fact of incidence. So very many women suffer male sexual violence, so very many men---ordinary men--are sexually violent toward women and children, that most of us will encounter at least one and probably more of them at some time in our lives.

When we look at all these women's stories together, we come to two related conclusions. First, women learn about men's violence in a variety of ways, starting at an early age. They learn about violence directly at the hands of abusers, often in a number of forms and a number of circumstances. They learn about violence by witnessing men abuse other women--their mothers, sisters, daughters, female co-workers. They learn about violence by listening to cultural messages, by hearing the violence done to women dismissed, tolerated, condoned, supported and even celebrated by the abusers themselves, friends and relations, the authorities women turn to for help, and by our society and culture in general.

Second, we conclude that in learning about male violence in these various ways women learn a key lesson in femininity. Femininity is what women are supposed to be. It includes being weak, passive, vulnerable, and sexually available to men. The femininity lesson women learn in learning about male violence is that women are abusable, that it is normal and acceptable for men to abuse women, and that to be a woman is to be both a target of and responsible for male violence.

So now we come to the men. What the men who rape and batter and sexually abuse children and sexually harass and buy women's and children's bodies in prostitution and pornography have in common is that they are ordinary men. They are lawyers and doctors and police officers, teachers and loggers and garbage collectors. They are seventeen and seventy. They are our fathers and husbands, bosses and neighbours. They are not insane or abnormal. They are not exceptional.

What these men seem to expect or require of women more than anything is that they be sexual by each man's own definition, a definition often both shaped by and reflected in the lies of pornography. So one young man demands his girlfriend wear tight jeans, another man beats his wife for looking too attractive to other men. One man yells at the child he is sexually abusing "when are you going to get tits on you," another shaves a child's pubic hair and slaps her breasts because he's angry at her for growing up.

Men's definition of women's sexuality includes at least acceptance of abuse. Because for these men male sexuality is abusive, they assume women will accept abuse. A woman who doesn't is told by her boyfriend she's not "woman enough" if she can't take the pain. And sometimes men's definition of women's sexuality includes enjoyment of the abuse. A man wants to know if the child he has raped has "come," a man beats his wife and then wants to have sex, later using her compliance as "proof" she wanted to be beaten, a woman in prostitution fakes an orgasm to please a trick, maybe to distract him from beating her.

Words like obedience, submission, compliance and silence show up frequently in the pictures. Men have authority over women and expect that authority to be respected. It means they expect women to give them what they want--sex or babies or clean socks or supper on the table--often without being asked. Men make the rules and change the rules without notice. One morning he demands a soft-cooked egg, the next he throws it in her face. He demands she get a job to support him and then beats her for not being home. He orders her to wear revealing clothes when they go out and then accuses her of coming on to other men. He tells her not to let men touch her sexually and then shows her exactly what she's supposed to prevent.

The thread that runs through all these is control. Men expect to control women, to have power over a weaker and therefore abusable other. Often power over means owning the other, temporarily or permanently. When a man owns a woman or child he can do with her whatever he wants. He can make her into an object, a thing to be played with and discarded. He can keep her barely human and derive his sexual pleasure from humiliating her, from watching her shame. Whether he treats her as an object or as a person, he can vent his hatred of women on her by hurting and humiliating what for women in this culture is our most private and vulnerable aspect--our sexual beings.

In recognizing the commonalities of women's experiences of male sexual violence it is important not to lose sight of the differences. Very often context, especially the victim's relationship to her abuser, influences how she thinks and feels about what he does to her. Obviously, if one's first direct experience of male sexual violence is as an adult raped by a stranger one will view that experience differently than does a child regularly molested by her "loving" grandfather. So too the nature and duration of the abuse has influence: being sexually harassed in one job is different from being beaten unconscious frequently in the course of a twenty year marriage.

A concrete example of differences which emerge in women's experience of different forms of male violence has to do with fear. Whatever the form of violence they are subjected to women speak of fear and say that fear is exacerbated by the unpredictability of men's violence. In dating violence, wife assault, child sexual abuse, rape, and prostitution women also fear being killed, something not reported by women who are sexually harassed. The former have good reason to fear being killed, for the violence to which they are subjected often is life-threatening and the abusers sometimes say they will kill them. This is not the case for women who are sexually harassed. Those women do say, though, that after being sexually harassed they become physically afraid, afraid to walk to their cars, afraid to be alone with male co-workers. They learn from the sexual harassment to fear at least the potential of men's violence. Like the women who fear being killed, they learn to fear an escalation of men's violence.

These differences have important implications for the kinds of services feminists develop. Women who are battered may need protection, a safe and supportive place to be while they sort out their options. Children who are sexually abused may also need protection as well as help in finding a language to describe what has been done to them. Women who are raped generally don't say they need refuge but they may need information and support and advocacy in dealing with medical, police and court procedures. Women who are sexually harassed may need advocacy and organizing support in dealing with management and unions and human rights tribunals. Women escaping prostitution may need education and job training as well as counselling support in overcoming the effects of sexual abuse. These are only some of the more obvious examples.

Within specific forms of male violence there are also variations in women's experience. For example, some battered women say their experience taught them that all men are violent and that they are afraid to consider marrying again. Others anticipate having another relationship but say they have lost their romanticism or idealism about marriage. Similarly, as adults some child sexual abuse survivors continue to hate and fear their abusers while others dismiss them as wimps and jerks. Just as it is important to remember the differences among the issues so too must we keep in mind the variations in women's experience of each issue.

Acknowledging these differences and variations, we end this picture where we began: with the commonality of women and women's experience. Just as the men who do violence are ordinary men, the women who suffer violence are ordinary women. They are our mothers and sisters and co-workers and friends; the women we meet on the bus, at the grocery store, in our feminist action groups. They are not "other" than us, for the training they receive in femininity, in women's "proper place", is the training we all receive.

An act of sexual violence against one woman is an act of terrorism against all women. We use the word advisedly, fully conscious of its power and meaning. Part of how terrorism works is that while a whole population is targetted for violence, individual victims are selected at random. They may not even be selected per se, but simply be in the wrong place--on the wrong flight, in the wrong pub--at the wrong time. The effect of such randomness is to constrain all members of the population. The women in the pictures, the women who have directly suffered male sexual violence, are not different from those of us who have not. Because we are women we are all targets of men's violence. Because we are women we all struggle to reclaim our lives from the power of that violence.

The Texts

Hanmer, Jalna & Mary Maynard, eds. *Women, Violence and Social Control.* Atlantic Highlands, N.J.: Humanities Press International, 1987. 213 pages, indexed.

The articles in this anthology were first presented as papers at the 1985 Annual Conference of the British Sociological Association. The editors describe the book as a collection of the most recent feminist work in the area of gender and violence, and they identify six themes running through the articles:

1) Violence and its threat are common and inhibiting features of most women's lives.
2) The question: What is violence and how should it be conceptualized?
3) Justifications for broadening the connotations of violence, especially for including the fear or threat of violence as part of violence itself.
4) How violence against women is processed in the civil and criminal justice systems.
5) How men's violence is challenged and resisted.
6) Men and masculinity.

Of course, no one article speaks to every theme, nor does any one theme appear in every article. And, again of course, for our purposes some themes, and hence some articles, are more relevant than others.

As descriptions of women's experience of male violence articles by Jill Radford and Liz Kelly are particularly useful. Both articles are based on women's accounts. As Radford puts it, "the women interviewed were a group of very real women who were prepared to share personal and often very painful experiences."

The study described by Radford, referred to as the Wandsworth study after the London borough in which it was conducted, asked women about their experiences of men's violence in the previous year only. Thus it excludes, among many others, adult survivors' experience of child sexual abuse, women's childhood experiences of witnessing their mothers being battered, and the experiences of women who have escape battering relationships. Given our contention that women learn about male violence cumulatively, this is a serious limitation to the study.

On the other hand, the Wandsworth study did ask the women whether they had witnessed or known of violence against other women, a subject very often omitted in other studies. Also omitted from most studies is the experience of women of colour, whereas in Wandsworth nearly one third of the respondants are either black or Asian. Unfortunately, Radford's report of the study does not distinguish between racial and sexual attacks and harassment, so it is difficult to trace the relationship of racism and sexism in these women's experience. Still, their inclusion is an important and positive feature of the article and the study on which it is based.

Liz Kelly began her work with two premises: 1) that links exist between different forms of sexual violence; 2) that most women have experienced sexual violence in their lifetimes. In investigating these assumptions she evolved a concept of the continuum of sexual violence. This isn't an entirely new concept but Kelly's development of it provides a useful model for understanding women's experience. She identifies two features of a continuum crucial to its definition. First, all the events or experiences in a continuum have a common underlying characteristic. Second, those events or experiences form a continuous series and pass into one another. She goes on to say that a continuum should not be seen as a linear connection, nor should it be taken to infer relative degrees of seriousness.

Kelly reports she has used the continuum in talks given to community women's groups. She says many women have found it helpful in locating and understanding their own experience of sexual violence. Kelly's use of the concept is also helpful in tracing "the linking of the more common, everyday abuses women experience with the less common experiences labelled as crimes." In so doing, Kelly argues that a clear distinction between "victims" and other women cannot be made, that the differences of women's experiences of violence are differences of degree and not kind. She concludes: "The same logic applies to the definition of 'offenders'."

Three other articles describing women's experience help to extend the common understanding of the acts included in a definition of sexual violence. Sandra McNeill looks at indecent exposure from women's perspective. While "flashing" is often trivialized by men in our culture, McNeill reports women do take it seriously, especially because they cannot predict whether a flasher will be violent. Interestingly, McNeill says she anticipated women would say they feared being raped but found instead that at the time of the incidents women fear death. Other responses she reports include shock, anger, and guilt, shame or humiliation.

Caroline Ramazanoglu describes the "insults, leers, sneers, jokes, patronage, bullying, vocal violence and sexual harassment" commonly experienced by women in academic life. Her language is a delightful mixture of reasoned interpretation and feistiness and her work serves to expose a widespread but often hidden form of male violence and its structural supports.

Diane Hudson describes a horrifying form of institutionalized male violence in the interests of social control--psychosurgery. She argues that this so-called medical treatment is used most often against women and has as its expressed aim modifying women's behaviour, in particular to "assist" women to conform to their gender roles. The case studies Hudson cites are enraging. One woman's lesbianism was called a personality disorder and treated with drugs and shock therapy. She was diagnosed as "hostile and aggressive" toward the step-father who sexually assaulted her as a child. This woman killed herself rather than submit to a "brain operation." All of the women in the study had been physically, sexually or psychologically abused by men. Instead of condemning that violence and assisting women to understand their experience of it, psychiatry's response was to excise parts of their brains. In short, men's abuse of women is considered normal, women's reactions to abuse, whether anger or depression, are not considered normal and are "treated" with further violence.

All of the articles cited above at least mention the fear or threat of violence as one aspect of women's experience. Elizabeth Stanko takes up the subject directly. She describes the "precautionary strategies" women adopt to avoid male violence or simply to cope with feelings of insecurity which the ever-present threat of violence generates. She says for women these strategies are "a way of living in a male-dominated world," a world in which most women experience some form of male violence.

Taken together the articles in this collection make an important contribution to feminists' understanding of women's experience of male violence, of the function of violence as social control, and of the role of the state in perpetuating men's violent control of women. Most importantly, from our perspective, articles by Kelly, Radford, Stanko, and others including R. Emerson Dobash and Russell Dobash contribute to our understanding of the patterns of male violence in women's lives.

MacKinnon, Catharine A. *Feminism Unmodified: Discourses on Life and Law.* Cambridge: Harvard University Press, 1987. 315 pages, indexed.

This is one of the most exciting and challenging works of feminist theory published in recent years. The writing is graceful though of necessity often conceptually difficult--certainly not a book to be read in an afternoon. Because it is a collection of speeches, the tone of the book is one of pursuasion.

Within the context of this Guide the most significant contribution MacKinnon makes with this book is her discussions of the meaning of violence in women's lives. She says that the issues of rape, wife assault, sexual harassment, child sexual abuse, pornography and prostitution are interconnected and "form a distinctive pattern: the power of men over women in society." For women the reality of men's sexual violence is so great and ever-present that, says MacKinnon, "to be about to be raped is to be gender female in the process of going about life as usual." For women the experience of sexual violation is so common as to form "the meaning and content of femininity."

That meaning is not just experiential but social as well. Consider the frequency with which, as children and adults, women are sexually violated by men, strangers and loved ones. Then consider how those victims are treated by both institutions and society in general. Put those two together and one may conclude, as MacKinnon does, that "a woman is socially defined as a person who, whether or not she is or has been, can be treated in these ways by men at any time, and little, if anything, will be done about it."

The most insidious harm of this social definition is that

women share it, believe it as men believe it. MacKinnon argues that "sexual desire in women, at least in this culture, is socially constructed as that by which we come to want our own self-annihilation." In other words, because sexuality is socially learned, and because in our society women's subordination is eroticized, women as well as men come to want male dominance: "we get off on it to a degree, if nowhere near as much as men do." Linking experience and social definition, MacKinnon says that sexual exploitation and degradation for women "produce grateful complicity in exchange for survival.... The issue is not why women acquiesce but why we ever do anything but."

MacKinnon asserts that women's ability to resist male violence, individually and collectively, is limited by two things. First, experiencing sexual exploitation and degradation produces "self-loathing to the point of extinction of self, and it is respect for self that makes resistance conceivable." Second, for all women the strategies required to survive daily in a world of systematic and systemic male sexual violence are "exactly the opposite of what is required to change it." In short, both the potential and the reality of male sexual violence work to prevent women from fighting that violence. For all women, those who have been victims and those not yet victims, the result is terror. Living in terror means that the time and energy and skills women could use to change the world or simply to live our lives is instead taken up "trying to figure out how not to be next on the list."

The most conceptually difficult theme running through this collection concerns the relationship of sex and violence. MacKinnon argues that feminists have been misguided in describing rape, for example, as a crime of violence not sex. The argument is complex and not easily summarized but seems to revolve around two main points. First, she says that in failing to talk about rape as sex we fail to criticize what is done to women in what is called normal sex. Hence, implicitly we accept that what distinguishes rape from intercourse is the level of force or coercion involved; that what is rape is that which goes beyond the standard of the normal level of force. Second, she contends that men experience rape, child sexual abuse, etc. as sex. They derive sexual pleasure from acts of dominance and submission. In what will no doubt become the most oft-quoted line in the book MacKinnon sums up the argument by saying, "Violence is sex when it is practised as sex."

Part of what makes this argument problematic is an issue MacKinnon herself raises. She says that in asking whether rape, pornography and sexual harassment are matters of violence or of sexuality it is important to ask "to whom?" In other words, whose perspective or experience is being asked for? The question then becomes, regardless of how men experience rape, etc., do women experience these things as violence or as sex. Kathleen Barry argues that neither rape victims nor women in prostitution experience what is done to them as sex. Similarly, Lorenne Clark and Debra Lewis say that women experience rape as assault.

Nevertheless, MacKinnon's argument challenges us to re-think our conceptions of sex and violence both in meaning and in experience. Throughout the book she demands that we push at the boundaries of thought and action, boundaries imposed by men and by ourselves. And she inspires:

> Be more radical than anyone has ever been about the unknown, because what has never been asked is probably what we most need to know. Take the unknowable more seriously than anyone ever has, because most women have died without a trace; but invent the capacity to act, because otherwise women will continue to.

Stanko, Elizabeth A. *Intimate Intrusions: Women's Experience of Male Violence.* London: Routledge & Kegan Paul, 1985. 211 pages, indexed.

If you have money enough for only one book this year, buy this one. In readable fashion, Elizabeth Stanko draws together themes from a range of issues into a general description of women's "ordinary experience" of male violence. Her analysis is grounded in women's lives, supplemented with descriptions and analyses of other feminists.

Stanko's starting place is that "to be a woman--in most societies, in most eras--is to experience physical and/or sexual terrorism at the hands of men." This is the "commonness" of women's lives, what we share regardless of age or class or race or any other division. Like Liz Kelly and Kathleen Barry, Stanko argues that the separation of some women into the category "victim" objectifies women's experience of male violence, denies the commonality among sexually and/or physically assaulted women, and, most importantly, denies their "oneness" with all women.

Stanko develops this thesis first by describing women's experiences of four very common forms of male sexual violence: rape, wife assault, incest and sexual harassment. In each of these chapters women's voices come through strongly and Stanko's analysis is at once lucid and succinct. For example, in the chapter on incest--subtitled "Some of Us Learn as Children"-- she describes child sexual abuse as an adult male asserting his power and right to use a child sexually any way he pleases. She locates this power in "adult emotional and physical experience and in the trust male adults automatically receive within the family unit." Conversely, the female child is powerless precisely because she is female and a child. Stanko comments, "lessons which taught the female child to be helpful, nurturant, supportive, and loving are not advantages to stopping the assaults." The result is a life of terror, "a constant state of anxiety, coupled with the inability to predict when, where and in what form sexual intrusion will occur."

The unpredictability of male violence is a theme Stanko returns to repeatedly throughout the text. She says, for example, that "women are unable to predict, and thus unable to control, men's behaviour or anticipate when it might lead to violence." Women observe men's behaviour closely--monitoring footsteps behind them on the street, for example--in an attempt to anticipate and thus avoid male violence. Stanko says that as women we "plan our lives" around this unpredictability--choosing which street to walk on, "cooking the eggs the way the husband likes them," in short, becoming "specialists in survival through avoidance strategies." Unfortunately, none of these strategies are foolproof.

Stanko says that the women whose experiences she describes--women raped, battered, incestuously assaulted as children, sexually harassed at work--all "speak in similar voices." They speak of being treated as sexually available to men, of being humiliated and feeling ashamed, of being grateful to survive. Furthermore, much of what they say "describes what it means to be female." What it means to be female is to be seen by men as primarily or exclusively sexual beings, to experience men's threatening, intimidating, coercive and violent behaviour, to have that experience dismissed or to be blamed for it, and often to blame ourselves. To be female is to live in fear, constantly on guard against men's violence. As Stanko says, "to walk the streets warily at night is how we actually feel our femininity."

This is an enormously important book. It is profoundly respectful of women and women's efforts to survive in a world of men's violence. It names that violence for what it is: typical male behaviour, sanctioned by the male point of view which permeates the institutions and relations of our society. In describing women's experiences of male violence as ordinary, in tracing the commonalities of women's experiences and the oneness of all women in our vulnerability to men's threatening, violent and coercive behaviour, Stanko has made an immense contribution to feminists' understanding of the patterns of violence in the lives of girls and women.

Other Useful Texts

Barry, Kathleen. *Female Sexual Slavery.* New York: Avon Books, 1979. 325 pages, indexed.

Though Barry's focus in this book is prostitution, she discusses the commonality of women's experience of male violence and discusses sexual terrorism as a fact of all women's lives. See full annotation in the Prostitution section.

Dworkin, Andrea. *Right Wing Women.* New York: Perigee, 1983. 255 pages, indexed.

This is a powerful book which describes the centrality of forced sex to the system of male dominance and female submission. It presents a model of the condition of women with pornography at the centre, prostitution at the edge, and rape, battery, reproductive exploitation and economic exploitation as a circle of crimes in between. Perhaps most important, Dworkin argues that what binds both feminists and right wing women together is that we all come from a common base of powerlessness and that the fate of every woman is tied to the fate of all women, including those she personally dislikes and politically and morally abhors. She concludes that recognizing the fact of women's oneness is an essential "discipline" for feminism both in theory and in practice.

Guberman, Connie & Margie Wolfe, eds. *No Safe Place: Violence Against Women and Children.* Toronto, Women's Press, 1985. 161 pages, not indexed.

A Canadian anthology of feminist writers on child battery, wife assault, rape, child sexual assault, sexual harassment and pornography. In the Introduction the editors note some themes running through the articles--power and violence, social relations, the family--and say there are connections among the issues of violence, though they don't specify what. As an anthology the quality is mixed, but it remains one of the few texts to address the various forms of violence against women from a Canadian perspective.

Hanmer, Jalna & Sheila Saunders. *Well-Founded Fear: A Community Study of Violence to Women.* **London: Hutchinson, 1984. 112 pages, not indexed.**

This book describes a community study of women's perceptions and experiences of male violence, conducted in Leeds, England in 1981. Also describes women's experience of police response to male violence. In spite of some methodological problems similar to those of the Wandsworth study, the text provides valuable information about women's experience and offers a useful analysis of the relationship of women's fear, social control, susceptibility to "private" violence and institutional responses.

Ridington, Jillian. *Beating the "Odds": Violence and Women With Disabilities.* **Toronto: DAWN Canada, 1989. 45 pages, not indexed.**

The issues which confront all women--vulnerability to male violence, isolation, lack of support services--are greatly compounded for women with disabilities. This position paper describes and analyses Canadian disabled women's experience of a number of forms of male violence, especially wife assault and child sexual abuse, and describes the obstacles those women face in trying to halt the violence. The author says "feminists are only just beginning to recognize that no woman can achieve security and equality until all women--including women with disabilities--are safe and equal." This book makes a valuable contribution to advancing that recognition. Its large print format makes it accessible to visually impaired women.

Russell, Diana E. H. & Nicole Van de Ven, eds. *Crimes Against Women: Proceedings of the International Tribunal.* **Millbrae, California: Les Femmes, 1976. 298 pages, not indexed.**

An amazing collection of testimonies from around the world. The crimes described include what we have called violence against women--rape, wife battering, etc.--plus a range of other crimes, including compulsory heterosexuality, forced sterilization, forced motherhood, economic crimes and on and on. Though somewhat old and, of necessity, brief in its description and analysis of each issue, the book is still an excellent international survey.

Postscript

Reading about men's violence against women is hard. Those of us who have experienced male violence, that is, most of us, may find that reading about other women's experiences triggers painful memories of our own assaults. Those of us who so far have avoided male violence may be concerned that learning about it will only feed our fear, that we can feel safe only if we don't know the possibilities. We may be worried that learning too much will make us hopeless or that we will come to hate men. We may simply shy away from knowledge which is painful, horrifying, or enraging.

But as hard as it is to read about men's violence against women, living with it is a lot harder. Each time we are tempted to avert our eyes we need to remember the women who don't have that option. When we want to put down a book about rape and watch television instead, we need to remember the children and women who can't avoid their knowledge because it is first hand. When we wish we could forget we'd ever heard of wife assault we need to remember the women who can't forget. When we want to remain ignorant we must remember our own experiences of being treated with disbelief by others who didn't want to know.

Yes, it is hard, but there is another side to the learning. The stories of men's violence are also stories of women's survival. Women do survive in the literal sense: they outlive the violence done to them. They do what Linda Marchiano did: they endure while they have to, escape when they can, and live beyond the violence. Alone and with the support of feminist services such as transition houses, women find ways to overcome the consequences of what has been done to them.